Men's Daily Strength
180 Inspirational Devotions in 3 Minutes

By: Tony Mejia

ISBN: 979-8-8691-2319-0

**Other Books written by
Tony Mejía in English and Spanish**

English:
1. From The Streets to The Altar
2. A Journey to Redemption
3. Morning Blessings & Mercies
4. New Year, New You! Devotional
5. New Year New You! Devotional/ Journal
6. Men's Daily Strength

Spanish:
1. De Las Calles al Altar
2. El Camino A la Redención
3. Bendiciones y Misericordias de la Mañana
4. ¡Nuevo Año, Nuevo Tu! Devocional
5. ¡Nuevo Año, Nuevo Tu! Devocional/ Diario
6. Fuerza Diaria de Los Hombres

**Books written in English and Spanish by Heidy
Mejía (Tony Mejía) Wife**

English:
1. Beyond my Wounds
2. The Power of Forgiveness
3. Corazon Abierto

Spanish:
4. Mas Alla de Mis Heridas
5. El Poder del Perdón
6. Open Heart

Men's Daily Strength
180 Inspirational Devotions in 3 Minutes
By: Tony Mejia

THE POWER OF SURRENDER

"Blessed is the one who trusts in the Lord, whose
confidence is in him." - Jeremiah 17:7

It could be challenging to accept the power of
surrender in a culture that frequently prizes
independence and control. But this verse also serves
as a reminder of the many benefits we receive when
we put our faith and trust in the Lord.

Recognizing that God is the ultimate source of
wisdom and direction necessitates humility in order
to surrender to Him. It entails surrendering to His
perfect will and letting up of our own goals and
objectives. Letting go of our concerns and anxiety

and trusting that God will faithfully meet all of our needs is another aspect of surrendering to Him.

Giving yourself over to God allows us to access His boundless grace and strength. We give Him permission to work in and through us, forming our moral fiber and guiding us toward righteousness. Giving yourself over to God is a source of peace and strength, not a sign of weakness.

Today, let us keep in mind the strength of giving up. May we put all of our confidence in the Lord, knowing that He will faithfully lead us, bless us, and grant our deepest aspirations.

ACCEPTING YOUR IDENTITY IN CHRIST

"Therefore, if anyone is in Christ, the new creation has come: The old has gone, the new is here!" - 2 Corinthians 5:17

Have you ever had trouble embracing who you are in Christ? Maybe self-talk that talks down to you, past transgressions, or outside pressures have made you question who you really are in Him. But keep in mind that we have undergone a significant transformation as Christ's followers.

We are reminded that we are new creations when we come into relationship with Jesus by the verse from 2 Corinthians 5:17. We are given a new beginning and the old, with all of its baggage and brokenness, is washed away. No longer do our transgressions, history, or flaws define us. Rather, Christ is where we find our actual identity.

Adopting the reality that we are whole, forgiven, and loved in Christ is the first step in accepting who we are. It entails accepting the veracity of God's Word and letting go of the labels and falsehoods the outside world attempts to impose on us.

Think for a moment today on who you are in Christ. Remember that He has chosen, redeemed, and accepted you. Give up any false beliefs about who you are, and accept the reality of who you are in Christ. Accept this new creation and allow it to influence your words, deeds, and mindset. You are called to an abundant life in Him and are valuable and cherished.

USING GOD'S WISDOM TO NAVIGATE DIFFICULTIES

"Trust in the LORD with all your heart, and do not lean on your own understanding." - Proverbs 3:5 (ESV)

There are many obstacles and hurdles in life that can quickly get to us. It's easy to lean on our own knowledge and seek answers based only on our own expertise when things are difficult. On the other hand, we are commanded to put all of our confidence in the Lord as men of faith.

The genius of God is beyond our comprehension. He understands what is best for us and has a broad perspective. Our human viewpoint is limited when we rely solely on our own understanding; however, when we put our trust in the Lord, we have access to His boundless wisdom.

It takes humility to navigate through challenges and to relinquish control. It entails admitting that we don't know everything and turning to the One who does to guide us. By putting our faith in the Lord, we give Him permission to direct our actions and give us the discernment we need to get through any obstacle.

Let us, as men, put all our confidence in the Lord, giving up our knowledge and seeking His counsel in all circumstances. As we face the challenges of life, may we find courage and guidance in Him, trusting that He is dependable and will lead us in the correct direction.

TRUSTING IN GOD AMIDST UNCERTAINTY

Proverbs 3:5-6 - "Trust in the Lord with all your heart and lean not on your own understanding; in all your ways submit to him, and he will make your paths straight."

It can be difficult to navigate through life's decisions and problems in an unpredictable environment. We could frequently find ourselves in a state of overwhelm and uncertainty. God, however, gives us a timeless promise: to put our trust in Him—even in the middle of this uncertainty.

We are reminded to rely on God's wisdom instead of our own understanding in Proverbs 3:5–6.

It is simple to rely on our own ideas and intentions, but sometimes the way that seems sense to us turns out not to be the best one. Rather, we are obligated to give up our ways and follow God's direction.

It might be challenging to fully trust in God, particularly when we are unable to comprehend His purposes or see the big picture. However, He promises to straighten our paths if we give up control and put our faith in Him. God knows what is best for us because He has a larger perspective. He will lead us through life's uncertainties by giving us clarity, serenity, and direction.

Let us put all our trust in the Lord during these uncertain times. We may rely on His wisdom and surrender our ways to Him, confident that He will guide us down the correct path. During life's uncertainty, may we find solace, serenity, and unwavering faith in God.

DEVELOPING AN APPRECIATIVE HEART

"Give thanks to the Lord, for he is good; his love endures forever." - Psalm 107:1

It might be simple to lose sight of the gifts and goodness that are all around us every day in a world that frequently concentrates on what we lack or what we desire. A deliberate effort and a change in viewpoint are necessary to cultivate a grateful heart. The Bible tells us to thank the Lord because He is good, and His love never ends.

When we practice thankfulness, we start to recognize God's faithfulness in the little things in life. We come to understand His protection, provision, and innumerable blessings—many of which we may have taken for granted. Experiencing gratitude allows us to see the beauty in every circumstance, especially during difficult times.

Men are expected to lead with a spirit of gratitude, serving as role models for our families and communities. True joy can be felt in any situation when we choose to concentrate on our blessings rather than our troubles. Let's cultivate the everyday habit of thanking God and recognizing His unwavering love and goodness.

THE DAILY STRENGTH OF PRAYER'S POWER

"Do not be anxious about anything, but in every situation, by prayer and petition, with thanksgiving, present your requests to God." - Philippians 4:6 (NIV)

It is simple to undervalue the power of prayer in our hectic lives. We frequently find ourselves fighting to overcome obstacles in life and relying solely on our own strength. But in Philippians 4:6, God reminds us that we should bring everything to Him in prayer rather than worrying.

Prayer is a tremendous source of strength and a way to connect with God; it is not a passive effort.

We demonstrate our faith and reliance on His heavenly direction and supply when we bring our requests before Him. We can release our anxieties and concerns through prayer because we know that God is in charge.

We develop a close relationship with our Heavenly Father via prayer. We can find consolation, serenity, and the fortitude to face any challenge in His presence. Through prayer, God may act in miraculous ways that change our weaknesses into His strength and our fears into calm.

Therefore, let us not undervalue the strength that comes from prayer on a daily basis. Let us make it a practice to go to God for guidance, to pour out our hearts to Him, and to observe His steadfast answer. We find comfort, discernment, and the superhuman strength to face every day with a fresh sense of hope and assurance in prayer.

OVERCOMING FAITH AND FEAR

Matthew 14:30-31 - "But when he saw the wind, he was afraid, and beginning to sink he cried out, 'Lord, save me.' Jesus immediately reached out his hand and took hold of him, saying to him, 'O you of little faith, why did you doubt?'"

We occasionally encounter circumstances in life that try our faith and awaken our worst anxieties. The account of Peter walking on water demonstrates how easily fear can overpower our faith. At first, Peter got out of the boat with whole faith and trust in Jesus. But anxiety set in when he noticed the wind and the waves, and he started to sink.

Similarly, we frequently encounter tumultuous situations that cause us to doubt and query God's existence and authority. We must never forget to call out to the Lord in these circumstances, just as Peter did. God is ever-present, ready to extend His hand and deliver us from our uncertainties and anxieties.

Unwavering trust is necessary to overcome fear. Jesus, the creator, and consummate form of our faith is the one we must keep our focus on. Let's decide to concentrate on His constancy, love, and promises whenever to worry rears its head. In prayer, let us give Him our worries, knowing that He will see us through every storm.

Let's strengthen our trust today by reflecting on the instances in which God has proven to be dependable and rescuing in our lives. Knowing that God is constantly by our side, ready to support us in overcoming our anxieties, let's choose to walk in trust and bravery. Fear will no longer be able to immobilize us if faith is our pillar; instead, we will overcome it and experience the freedom and serenity that is exclusive to God.

BUILDING RESILIENCE THROUGH GOD'S WORD

"But his delight is in the law of the Lord, and in His law, he meditates day and night." - Psalm 1:2

We encounter numerous difficulties in life that have the potential to weaken our will and faith. We frequently turn to prayer for comfort and encouragement, which is essential to our connection with God. But occasionally, we could feel cut off from God or find it difficult to find the right words to say in prayer. God's Word can help us develop resilience in difficult situations.

We are reminded in Psalm 1:2 of the value of taking pleasure in and reflecting on the Lord's law day and night. God's Word provides us with knowledge and direction that can strengthen our hearts and brains when we immerse ourselves in it. The Bible is replete with tales of men and women who overcame overwhelming obstacles and discovered strength in God's Word.

We open the door to receiving direct communication from God when we consistently read and study the Bible. His Word turns into a source of consolation, inspiration, and guidance. By meditating on His promises and precepts, we can develop resilience in all facets of our lives and weather life's storms.

Let's resolve to spend time in God's Word today, even if it seems tough to pray. God's truth will empower us to meet any difficulty and assist us in developing steadfast resilience as we give our hearts to the Scriptures.

DISCOVERING JOY IN THE ORDINARY

"There is nothing better for a person than that he
should eat and drink and find enjoyment in his toil."
- Ecclesiastes 2:24

It is simple to become engrossed in the chase of significant achievements and unique experiences amidst the daily chaos. We frequently lose sight of the joy that can be found in life's everyday moments as we race after achievement and look for fulfillment in the unusual.

However, the Bible reminds us that even the most basic activities, like eating and drinking, can provide beauty and happiness. God invites us to find contentment in the routine duties that comprise our life and to appreciate the commonplace. We have a greater sense of contentment and delight when we approach these times with an attitude of gratitude and awareness.

Let's take a moment to be grateful for the little things that God has given us rather than constantly aiming for the next big thing. Let us find happiness in the ordinary, the regular, and the seemingly small moments. When we do this, we will discover true contentment in the mundane and our hearts will be overflowing with thankfulness.

THE SIGNIFICANCE OF POSITIVE RELATIONSHIPS

"Walk with the wise and become wise, for a companion of fools suffers harm," reads Proverbs 13:20

In a society that frequently encourages independence and self-reliance, it's simple to undervalue the significance of healthy connections in our lives. But the Bible also emphasizes how important it is to develop positive relationships with other people.

We receive accountability, support, and inspiration from positive connections. They serve as a reminder of the value of community and the strength of unanimity. We foster an atmosphere where we can all advance in holiness together when we interact with others who uphold the same values and beliefs.

Furthermore, fulfilling relationships show God's love for us. We become vessels of His grace and love when we truly care for and assist others. We can alter, comfort, and give hope to people around us through our connections.

Think about the relationships in your life for a moment. Are they inspiring, uplifted, and uplifting? Are there any detrimental factors that require attention? Accept the importance of healthy relationships and make a conscious effort to cultivate bonds that are in line with God's desire. You will feel more fulfilled and purposeful in your spiritual path as you walk with the wise and seek connections that are centered on God.

GUARDING YOUR HEART: FINDING STRENGTH IN GOD'S WORD

Proverbs 4:23 (NIV) - "Above all else, guard your
heart, for everything you do flows from it."

It might be difficult for males to get past the
pressures and diversions that surround us in a world
full with temptations. But as Christ-followers, we are
obligated to guard our hearts and turn to God's Word
for support.

We are reminded in Proverbs 4:23 of the value
of guarding our hearts since they are the source of
life. Everything that comes into our minds, words,
and bodies originates in our hearts. Temptations have

the power to contaminate our entire existence if we let them into our hearts.

Recognizing our vulnerability is the first step toward conquering temptation. It is via this humility that we can ask God for help and discernment in navigating the perilous paths that lie ahead of us. Spending a lot of time in His Word gives us the wisdom and direction we need to make moral choices.

Let us look to God's Word as our strength when we are tempted. Consider reading passages that serve as a reminder of God's grace and promises. Seek accountability via prayer and relationships with other Christians who can support and uplift us when we stray from the road.

Let us rigorously protect our hearts today and rely on God's help to resist the temptations that are in front of us. With His help and might, we are able to remain firm and honor Him in every aspect of our lives.

Recall that you are not fighting temptation by yourself. God is with us, giving us the tools we need to triumph and the ability to live a life that exalts His name.

FINDING MEANING IN YOUR WORK

Ecclesiastes 2:24 (NIV)
"A person can do nothing better than to eat and
drink and find satisfaction in their own toil. This
too, I see, is from the hand of God."

Work frequently becomes a means to a goal in our culture. We Labor Day in and day out, just thinking about the material comforts that come with our paychecks. But we are called, as men of God, to look deeper for the purpose of our job.

God gave us the ability to express our gifts, benefit society, and feel gratified by our labors when He created work. But far too frequently, we make the mistake of looking for fulfillment in material accomplishments rather than in God's plan for our lives.

The Ecclesiastes passage serves as a reminder that real fulfillment and significance in our job arise when we recognize that it is a gift from God. The commonplace task of labor becomes a worthwhile undertaking when we see it as a means of serving others and exalting Him.

Let us endeavor to find happiness in our labors today, understanding that our labor serves a greater good than ourselves. Let's beg God to reveal His plan for our lives and seek His wisdom and direction for our jobs. May we find satisfaction in the job itself as well as in the outcomes, understanding that each task we complete with a heart devoted to God moves us one step closer to realizing our purpose in Him.

MANAGING STRESS WITH GOD'S CALM

"Be still before the Lord and wait patiently for him; do not fret when people succeed in their ways, when they carry out their wicked schemes." - Psalm 37:7

Life can frequently be too much to handle, with a lot of stress, obligations, and unforeseen difficulties. It could seem impossible to find serenity and tranquility in the middle of it all. But we are not called to manage stress on our own as men of faith. God gives us His serenity, His presence, and His direction.

When faced with difficult events in this fast-paced world, we might be inclined to react impulsively or make snap decisions. But God tells us to remain motionless and to patiently await His arrival. We can keep ourselves and other people safe by asking for His guidance and wisdom before making decisions. God desires for us to have faith in Him, understanding that He is in control of everything.

Let's give our worries to the Lord when we feel like tension will get the better of us. Let us put our attention on God's sovereignty and His plan for our lives, instead of worrying about the accomplishments and schemes of others. His serenity may center our hearts and thoughts, giving us the fortitude and resiliency to handle stress with poise.

Let's keep in mind today that we don't have to handle tension on our own. Seek God's counsel, put your trust in His serenity, and invite God into every situation. With God at our side, we will be able to conquer tension and find serenity in the middle of the chaos.

ACCEPTING THE GRACE OF GOD DESPITE IMPERFECTION

"But he said to me, 'My grace is sufficient for you, for my power is made perfect in weakness.'" - 2 Corinthians 12:9

It can be easy for us males to feel overwhelmed by our own flaws and weaknesses in a world that frequently demands perfection. Even if we try our hardest to be better friends, spouses, dads, and leaders, we occasionally fail. We falter, we fall, we make mistakes.

But there is grace even in our imperfections. God's grace is independent of our competence or sense of self-worth. In actuality, His power is perfected in our weakness. Our errors don't have to be the burden we bear alone. We don't need to put on a front of flawlessness. Alternatively, we could gratefully embrace God's grace.

All of our flaws are sufficiently covered by God's grace. We are able to discover strength, healing, and forgiveness because of His grace. Let's accept our shortcomings and let God's grace operate in and through us rather than aiming for perfection. By doing this, we will encounter God's transforming force, which has the capacity to change our weaknesses into our strengths.

MAINTAINING YOUR STRENGTH IN THE FACE OF MISERY

Isaiah 40:31 - "but those who hope in the Lord will renew their strength. They will soar on wings like eagles; they will run and not grow weary, they will walk and not be faint."

There are a lot of obstacles in life that might make us feel depressed and worn out. These are the moments when we could doubt our perseverance and wonder how we can go on. But as men of faith, we possess a strength that transcends both our circumstances and physical capabilities.

We are reminded of the significance of putting our hope in the Lord in Isaiah 40:31. He will replenish our strength when we put our faith in Him. He gives us the ability to run with endurance, walk without becoming tired, and soar above our situations like eagles.

It's critical that we never forget that the Lord is the source of our strength when we are faced with suffering. He is our haven and the one who gives us the strength to endure even in the most trying circumstances.

Let us make the decision to stay strong today by focusing on God and putting our hope in Him. As we do, we can have faith that He will never abandon us and will give us the courage to endure any trial or suffering that comes our way.

THE WILLINGNESS TO PARDON AND MEND

"But I tell you, love your enemies and pray for those who persecute you." - Matthew 5:44

Has someone ever harmed or deceived you? It's normal to be offended or resentful of people who have harmed us. However, we are expected to a higher standard as Christ's disciples. Even our adversaries deserve our compassion and forgiveness.

Jesus teaches us the value of forgiveness and love in Matthew 5:44. He urges us to love our adversaries and those who persecute us in addition to our friends and family. Even though it can appear impossible, we can discover the strength to do this duty by the power of the Holy Spirit.

We release ourselves from the weight of resentment and bitterness when we choose to love and forgive those who have wronged us. We give God permission to heal our wounded hearts and reconcile our spirits. Though it's not always simple, when we choose love over hate, we honor God and emulate the qualities of Christ.

Let's look into our hearts today and beg God to grant us the capacity to forgive and heal. As God has done for us, let us pray for those who have harmed us and show them forgiveness and mercy. May we feel the freedom that comes from letting go and accepting forgiveness, and may our love serve as a testament to God's transformative power.

SEEKING GOD'S INSIGHT WHILE MAKING DECISIONS

"Trust in the LORD with all your heart and lean not on your own understanding; in all your ways submit to him, and he will make your paths straight" - Proverbs 3:5-6

Men are frequently forced to make crucial choices that have the power to alter the trajectory of their lives. It is essential that we ask God for wisdom and direction during these times. Scripture urges us to put all of our reliance in the Lord, even when the outside world may urge us to rely on our own judgment or take other people's advice.

When we put our faith in God, we confess that His wisdom is greater than our own finite comprehension. He wants to guide us along the correct path and is aware of the plans He has for us. Seeking God's wisdom, however, entails more than just accepting His knowledge; it also entails submitting our own plans and aspirations to His will.

Let us approach God in humility during the decision-making process, asking for His direction via prayer and His Word. Let's be willing to follow the Holy Spirit's guidance and put our trust in His wisdom. We may rely on God to guide us and straighten our paths as we accomplish this, bringing us to the abundant life He has promised.

LEADING AN HONEST LIFE

Proverbs 11:3 - "The integrity of the upright guides them, but the unfaithful are destroyed by their duplicity."

It might be simple to give in to the temptations of dishonesty and deceit in a society that frequently prizes success at any cost. On the other hand, we are expected to live honorable and truthful lives as men of God. Today's verse serves as a helpful reminder of how important living an honest life is.

The upright are guided by integrity. Our moral compass is what guides our choices and deeds. We are resistant to the pressures of this world when we choose to walk in honesty. A higher standard that embodies the nature of our Heavenly Father serves as our guide.

However, because of their deceit, individuals who are unfaithful and dishonest risk annihilation. At first, the road of dishonesty could seem alluring since it offers speedy rewards and short cuts to achievement. However, it ultimately results in devastation and emptiness.

We are expected to be different as men of God. Let's resolve to live honorable lives and ask the Lord for guidance in all that we do. By doing this, we reflect the nature of our Heavenly Father and become a light in a dark world. May we always maintain our moral standards, understanding that God rewards those who live moral lives.

CULTIVATING POSITIVE CONNECTIONS

Proverbs 13:20 (NIV) - "Walk with the wise and become wise, for a companion of fools suffers harm."

It is critical for us as guys to surround ourselves with positive people in a world full of negativity and distractions. The people we select to surround ourselves with greatly influence our decisions, character, and state of mind. Men who aspire to live godly lives need to intentionally cultivate relationships that uplift and support our quest for insight.

Proverbs 13:20 serves as a reminder of the significant impact our friends and family have on us.

Making sensible decisions and gaining wisdom are made possible by walking among the wise. On the other hand, associating with idiotic people might cause harm and unfavorable outcomes.

We must ask God for wisdom and discernment in our relationships as we work to build healthy bonds. Let us surround ourselves with people who uphold our moral principles, push us to grow as people, and mirror the truth and love of God.

Consider the individuals in your life for a moment today. Do they guide you in the wrong directions or are they a source of wisdom and support? Seek God's assistance in recognizing and cultivating relationships that will strengthen your faith and moral fiber.

Remember that we can experience spiritual enrichment, growth, and accountability by surrounding ourselves with wise company and pursuing godly connections. May our relationships eventually exalt God's name and be in line with His plan for us.

THE GRACE OF GOD'S PEACE

Philippians 4:7 - "And the peace of God, which surpasses all understanding, will guard your hearts and your minds in Christ Jesus."

In a chaotic and uncertain world, finding tranquility might sometimes seem unattainable. The demands of our daily lives, our relationships, and our jobs can exhaust and overwhelm us. However, as men of faith, we have access to God's peace, which is greater than any human comprehension.

God's grace of peace is independent of our situation or our capacity to influence it. It is an ethereal calm that envelops our hearts and brains, protecting us from uncertainty, fear, and anxiety. We can experience this tranquility because of our relationship with Christ Jesus.

God's peace is a need, not an extravagance. It offers us hope when all else appears lost and keeps us going through difficult times. It is a tranquility that is beyond our comprehension, based on the conviction that God is in charge and is using everything for our benefit.

Let's give God our concerns and fears today so we can welcome His serenity. Having peace that guards our hearts and minds, let us believe that His grace is enough to get us through each day. May we take comfort in the unwavering reality that we can always access God's peace, no matter what our situation.

FACING ANGER WITH GOD'S LOVE

Ephesians 4:26-27 - "In your anger do not sin": Do not let the sun go down while you are still angry, and do not give the devil a foothold.

Anger is a strong feeling that may easily take over our hearts and cause us to make terrible choices. Although everyone experiences times of irritation and disappointment, how we handle these emotions can have a significant effect on both our relationships and our relationship with God.

Paul exhorts us not to let our rage to grow and fester overnight in Ephesians 4:26–27. It's simple to let resentment fester and build, but when we do, we give the devil access to our lives. Instead, we must promptly deal with our anger by giving it to God and seeking His insight.

Let us keep in mind Jesus' example when we are angry. He rejected vengeance and hatred in favor of compassion and forgiving. It is our duty as His disciples to emulate Him. We can look to God's Word during trying times to find His love and direction for managing our emotions.

Let's open our hearts to receive God's love today so that we can react to wrath with forgiveness, grace, and mercy. May we decide to let go of our resentment and let His love direct our behavior. By doing this, we can stay away from sin and walk in His love, showing the world what kind of person, He is.

TURNING TRIALS INTO TRIUMPHS

James 1:2-4 (NIV) - "Consider it pure joy, my brothers and sisters, whenever you face trials of many kinds, because you know that the testing of your faith produces perseverance. Let perseverance finish its work so that you may be mature and complete, not lacking anything."

We all face challenges and hardships in life that have the power to completely devastate us. It might be simple to feel defeated, despondent, and overwhelmed during these times. This verse, however, serves as a compelling reminder of the possibility that our struggles will ultimately result in victories.

We are called to welcome our trials with enthusiasm and consider them as chances for personal development, rather than seeing them as merely sources of suffering. We grow in perseverance when our faith is put to the test. We become stronger, more mature people as a result of overcoming these adversities.

God shapes our character, refines us, and increases our reliance on Him via our hardships. He gives us the courage and discernment to face our challenges head-on when we give them over to Him. Our struggles turn into opportunities for triumph, evidence of God's fidelity, and windows through which His splendor can be seen.

Thus, let us not let the difficulties we encounter depress us. Rather, let us believe that God is at work in and through them, and that if we persevere and put our trust in Him, He will finally bring about our victory. Put your hope and trust in the One who has the power to work out every circumstance for your benefit, and transform your trials into victories.

THE CALL TO LEAD WITH HUMILITY

"Whoever wants to become great among you must be your servant, and whoever wants to be first must be slave of all." - Mark 10:43-44

Men tend to equate leadership with having authority, power, and recognition. We want to be at the top, to be regarded as influential and successful. Jesus, however, challenges us to a different form of leadership—one that is based on service and humility.

Being a slave or a servant may appear to be a sign of weakness to the outside world, but Jesus challenges this idea. He teaches us that helping others, putting their needs ahead of our own, and exercising humility in leadership are the keys to real greatness.

We must put our own egos and pride aside to lead with humility. It entails listening intently, obtaining informed advice, and prioritizing the needs of others over our own. It entails setting a good example, being kind and compassionate, and being prepared to put in the extra effort required to help people around us.

We become more receptive to God's compassion and kindness when we accept the challenge to lead with humility. We turn into conduits for His love to be shown to others. In a world that so urgently needs His touch, we take on the role of being Jesus' hands and feet.

Let's reexamine what leadership means today and accept the call to service. Knowing that true greatness lies in selflessness, compassion, and a willingness to put others before ourselves, let us lead with humility. May serving others, as our Savior, Jesus Christ, exemplifies, provide us happiness and meaning.

EMBRACING GOD'S PROMISES FOR PROVISION

"But my God shall supply all your need according to his riches in glory by Christ Jesus." - Philippians 4:19

It's simple to get worried about our provision and material wants in a society where things are unclear and often changing. But we are commanded, as men of faith, to put our faith in God's promises of supply.

The Bible serves as a reminder that God is our ultimate provider. He pledges to meet all our needs, not in accordance with our meager means but rather in accordance with His immeasurable riches and majesty. This verse serves as a reminder that via

51

Christ Jesus, we are provided for from the bountiful storehouses of heaven.

Accepting God's promises of provision necessitates a change in viewpoint and a strong dependence on Him. We are asked to give God our anxieties and fears, believing that He would provide for us in ways that are beyond our comprehension, rather of depending just on our own resources and efforts.

Let us accept God's promises of provision as men of faith. Seeking His direction, working hard, and having faith that He will provide for our needs in His perfect time and manner are all that is required. May the knowledge that our heavenly father watches over us and is dependable in meeting all of our needs bring us comfort and joy.

RELYING ON GOD'S STRENGTH IN WEAKNESS

"Blessed be the God and Father of our Lord Jesus Christ, the Father of mercies and God of all comfort, who comforts us in all our affliction, so that we may be able to comfort those who are in any affliction, with the comfort with which we ourselves are comforted by God." (2 Corinthians 1:3-4)

Numerous obstacles may come our way in life. We may experience overwhelming feelings of helplessness and loneliness during these periods of weakness and hardship. But as men of faith, we must keep in mind that we are not limited to depending only on our own might. God is always available to offer courage, support, and direction. He is the Father of mercies and consolation.

God's reassuring and loving presence gives us strength amid our frailty. He is prepared to provide His boundless grace because He recognizes our difficulties. We make room for God to act in and through us when we turn our attention from ourselves and toward Him. We become conduits for His consolation, equipped to serve those facing like difficulties.

Brothers let's not give up or allow our shortcomings depress us. Rather, let us rely on God and believe in His dependable power. As we do, we will feel His consolation and be able to share it with others who are grieving. May we trust in God's might, understanding that we are never in this battle alone.

THE IMPACT OF A GRACIOUS HEART

In Proverbs 11:16, we read these words of wisdom: "A gracious woman gets honor, and violent men get riches."

It's simple to underestimate the influence of a grateful heart in a society that frequently prizes conceit and self-aggrandizement. Nonetheless, the Bible serves as a constant reminder of the life-changing power that love and kindness can have on both the people around us and ourselves.

God's heart is reflected in us when we approach people with grace. Our compassion and gentleness can make someone feel comfortable enough to open up and ask for help. In their lives, we act as conduits for God's love and His transformation.

Furthermore, we benefit and grow personally when we practice having a kind heart. This is so that God can work in and through us when we perform deeds of mercy and kindness because they come from a position of humility and selflessness. When we show grace, we make room for grace to come back to us.

Thus, let us try to live kindly and ask God for direction in all of our dealings. May people around us find solace, healing, and transformation from our words and deeds. Recall that having a grateful heart has the power to positively touch people's lives and have a wide-ranging effect.

FAITH-STRENGTHENING THROUGH GOD'S WORD

"So then faith comes by hearing, and hearing by the word of God." - Romans 10:17

Our faith might become brittle and feeble in an uncertain world. We must look to God's Word, the ultimate source of support and direction, during these trying times. The Bible is a living, powerful tool that may change our lives and fortify our faith; it is more than just a collection of tales and proverbial wisdom.

We are reminded in Romans 10:17 that hearing God's Word is the source of faith. Our faith grows and flourishes as we spend time reading, studying, and thinking about Scripture. God's Word has the capacity to rekindle our faith, revitalize our thoughts, and give us self-assurance.

However, reading the Bible on its own is insufficient; we also need to actively interact with it and let it into our souls. God makes Himself known to us via the promises, directions, and realities included in His Word. We receive consolation in difficult times, discernment in making choices, and inspiration to seek righteousness from His Word.

Let us prioritize seeking God's Word above anything else today. Let us thirst for His word, consider His promises, and put His lessons into practice in our daily lives. As we do this, God's Word will become more powerful in our lives and our faith will grow stronger. May we walk in obedience to His truth, with our hearts wide open to receive it.

IN THE ARENA: OVERCOMING CHALLENGES WITH GOD'S STRENGTH

In 2 Corinthians 12:9, it says, "But he said to me, 'My grace is sufficient for you, for my power is made perfect in weakness.'"

There are many obstacles in life, and sometimes it seems like we are fighting an uphill battle. We could experience overpowering issues in our personal lives, relationships, or places of employment. It is simple to feel frustrated and like giving up during these times.

However, we are called to a different viewpoint as men of faith. It's not just us that face difficulties. As a matter of fact, we possess the strength of God.

Rather of attempting to manage everything ourselves, we must humble ourselves and turn to God for direction and assistance. He has assured us that he will give us the fortitude to overcome every obstacle in our path.

Therefore, let us not let the difficulties we face deter us. Rather, let us rely on God and His strength to get us through the challenges of life. Recall that we are able to conquer every obstacle in our path because of His strength.

FINDING PURPOSE IN SERVING OTHERS

Mark 10:45 (NIV)
"For even the Son of Man did not come to be served, but to serve, and to give his life as a ransom for many."

Men frequently find themselves aiming for reputation, money, and success. We are inundated with messages telling us to prioritize our own needs and put ourselves first. We are called to a new way of life, nonetheless, in the middle of this world where everyone is self-centered.

Jesus reminds us of His mission on earth in Mark 10:45. He came to serve, not to be served. He voluntarily gave up His life to save others. This verse pushes us to change our viewpoint and discover meaning in helping others.

It might not always come easily to us to serve others. We might have to give up our comfort, finances, and time for it. However, we align ourselves with the heart when we choose to serve.

Beyond our personal goals, serving others enables us to discover contentment, joy, and meaning. It enables us to significantly impact the lives of those in our immediate vicinity. There are many ways we may help, such working at a nearby charity, mentoring a young person, or just being a listening ear.

Let's pray to God to help us see the needs in our community and to give us the bravery to go help others. May we discover our ultimate goal by imitating Jesus, who offered His life in order to save us. Not only does assisting others improve their lives, but it also exalts God.

SURRENDERING TO GOD'S WILL: IDENTIFYING STRENGTH IN TRUST

"Blessed is the man who trusts in the Lord, whose trust is the Lord." - Jeremiah 17:7 (ESV)

Giving oneself to God's will seem paradoxical in a society that prizes autonomy and self-sufficiency. It means putting our faith in the Lord and letting go of our own goals and objectives. However, as this scripture reminds us, putting our reliance in God gives us a lot of power.

Recognizing that the Lord's timing and intentions are far superior to our own is a necessary part of trusting in Him. It entails letting up of our desire for control and making the decision to have

63

faith that God is dependable and will lead us in the correct path. It calls for humility and a readiness to follow His direction.

Even if giving up could be difficult at times, it is this act of faith that leads to real strength. When we put our trust in God, we rely on His boundless power and knowledge rather than our own finite strength and wisdom. Knowing that God is arranging things for our benefit and that we are not alone in our decisions can bring us comfort.

Thus, let us submit to God's will and ask for His wisdom and direction in every aspect of our lives. May we recognize the power that comes from putting our faith in the Lord, knowing that He will be dependable in keeping His word and guiding us toward achievement and contentment.

THE FREEDOM OF SURRENDERED LIVING

"Therefore, I urge you, brothers and sisters, in view of God's mercy, to offer your bodies as a living sacrifice, holy and pleasing to God—this is your true and proper worship." Romans 12:1 (NIV)

Men frequently aspire to be independent and in charge of their lives. We want to be in control, to make our own choices and pursue our own goals. But when we give our life to God, we can finally experience the genuine freedom we seek.

The apostle Paul exhorts us to present our bodies to God as living sacrifices in this verse. This entails giving Him our free will, our goals, and our plans.

We can only truly experience freedom and life transformation via surrender.

Giving ourselves over to God enables us to let go of our problems and burdens because we have faith that He is aware of what is best for us. We are set free from the chains of sin and the burdensome efforts when we give up.

Men have the option to live lives of surrender, believing that God has good and perfect intentions for us. Let's surrender our egos and sense of power to God and let Him lead and guide us. True freedom and the wonderful life God has planned for us are found in surrender.

OVERCOMING WORRY WITH GOD'S PEACE

Philippians 4:6-7 - "Do not be anxious about anything, but in every situation, by prayer and petition, with thanksgiving, present your requests to God. And the peace of God, which transcends all understanding, will guard your hearts and your minds in Christ Jesus."

In a world full of unknowns and difficulties, it's simple to become overtaken by anxiety. Our worries can include things like our financial situation, relationships, future, and a host of other things. But as men of faith, we are urged to rise above anxiety and take advantage of God's serenity.

Philippians 4:6-7 serves as a helpful reminder to not worry about anything. Though it may be easier said than done, having faith in God is the key to overcoming anxiety. We are urged to submit our troubles to God in prayer, with thanksgiving, rather than letting them consume us. Our direct channel of contact with the universe's creator, who is aware of all of our needs and eager to assist us, is via prayer.

The moment we give our troubles to God, a miracle occurs. His calm, which is beyond our comprehension, permeates our hearts and thoughts. It's a tranquility that defies comprehension or explanation by human reason alone. This calm serves as a barrier against uncertainty, worry, and anxiety. It is the reassurance that God is in charge of our life and that we are not alone.

Men, we must always keep in mind that worrying does not make life any better. Rather, it robs us of happiness and undermines our faith. Let's make the decision to give God our worries today, trusting that He will take care of our needs and provide for our needs. Let's practice prayer and gratitude daily so that God's peace might rule in every circumstances. May His serenity guard our hearts and thoughts, giving us the strength to let go of anxiety and live in the liberty and assurance that come from putting our faith in Him.

Challenge: Spend a few minutes every day praying to God and bringing your concerns to Him. Express your worries to God in writing while giving Him thanks for His supply and faithfulness. You can overcome worry and enjoy God's abundant peace as you develop this habit of surrender, knowing that His peace will watch over your heart and mind.

USING YOUR FINANCES TO HONOR GOD

"Honor the Lord with your wealth and with the first fruits of all your produce." - Proverbs 3:9

We are obligated to glorify God with every part of our existence as men of God, including our financial situation. Our values and priorities can frequently be seen in how we relate to money. In the materialistic world of today, it's simple to become engrossed in the chase of material prosperity.

However, as the Bible reminds us, we have a responsibility to use our wealth to glorify the Lord. This entails managing our funds sensibly and in a way that honors and pleases God in addition to being good stewards of them.

Returning the first fruits of our produce to God is one way we can glorify Him with our money. This acknowledges that God is the source of all good things and is a symbol of obedience and trust. We express our thanks and dependence on Him by consistently paying our tithes and offerings.

Furthermore, we ought to utilize our money to further causes that are consistent with the principles of God's Kingdom. We may show that we are committed to honoring God with our financial lives by investing in missions, contributing liberally to the work of His church, and providing aid to those in need.

Instead of letting the chase of wealth consume us, let's use money to glorify God and further His Kingdom on earth. We will enjoy His blessings and the satisfaction of knowing that our resources are being used for His glory as we give Him top priority while making financial decisions.

THE POWER OF GOD'S UNWAVERING LOVE

Romans 8:38-39 - "For I am convinced that neither death nor life, neither angels nor demons, neither the present nor the future, nor any powers, neither height nor depth, nor anything else in all creation, will be able to separate us from the love of God that is in Christ Jesus our Lord."

It is consoling to know that God's love is unfailing and steadfast in a world full of uncertainty and perpetual change. He has love that is beyond comprehension; it is not based on our circumstances or our actions.

The knowledge that God's love for us is unchanging gives us comfort during any difficulties. It is a love that surpasses our inadequacies, fears, and failures. It is a love that endures despite our uncertainties and difficulties.

God's steadfast love has transformational power. It has the capacity to mend our brokenness, bolster our faith, and give us the strength to endure life's hardships. God's love for us is so great that it gives us the strength to face fear, go through trials, and confidently pursue His plan for our life.

Let today us consider the fact that nothing in all of creation—no situation, no person, no force in this world—can keep us from being loved by God. It is a love that never fades and that we can have every single day. We may be confident that God's love will support and lead us through every stage of life, regardless of the challenges we may encounter.

LEADING AN INTEGRAL LIFE

"Trust in the Lord with all your heart and lean not on your own understanding; in all your ways submit to him, and he will make your paths straight." - Proverbs 3:5-6

We are required to be men of integrity in a society that frequently promotes deceit and compromise. However, what does leading an integrative life entail?

Living an integral life entail putting all of our faith and confidence in the Lord and not in our own wisdom. It entails giving God all of our goals, plans, and aspirations and admitting that only He has the perfect insight to lead us in the correct direction.

Giving ourselves over to God in every way is another aspect of living an integrated life. This calls for humility and a readiness to ask for His wisdom and direction in all of our decisions. Let us constantly remember this when making decisions about our daily lives, occupations, and relationships seeking God's direction.

The Lord promises to make our pathways straight if we put our trust in Him and surrender to Him. He will lead us to a life filled with meaning and fulfillment, guard us, and guide us. Let us try to live honorably, going where God leads us in every area of our lives. May we be regarded as men who aim to please the Lord in whatever we do and who put our complete trust in Him.

HANDLING FAMILY DIFFICULTIES WITH FAITH

Proverbs 3:5-6 - "Trust in the Lord with all your heart and lean not on your own understanding; in all your ways submit to him, and he will make your paths straight."

Life can be full of challenges and hardships, particularly in our families. We might experience disagreements, miscommunications, or difficult relationships. It's simple to feel overwhelmed in these situations and to stop believing in God's purpose for our family.

But even during turmoil, the Bible exhorts us to put all our trust in the Lord. Because of the limitations of our knowledge, we might not always be able to understand the causes of the problems we encounter. But God promises to make our paths straight if we submit our ways to Him and rely on His wisdom.

It's critical to keep in mind that God is in charge when dealing with family issues. He understands what is best for us and our loved ones since he has a broad perspective. Rather than depending exclusively on our own capabilities and comprehension, we are obligated to have confidence in Him and pursue His direction.

THE BENEFITS OF GOD'S DIRECTION

Proverbs 3:6 - "In all your ways acknowledge him,
and he will make straight your paths."

Men frequently take great satisfaction in their independence and ability to reason and make decisions based only on their own intuition. Nonetheless, it is beneficial to look to God for guidance in every area of your life. He will straighten our paths if we acknowledge Him and give Him our goals and intentions.

Seeking God's guidance has several advantages. First, we are saved from the dangers of acting on impulse or haste, which might have unfavorable effects. God's guidance gives us the insight, wisdom, and clarity to make decisions that are in line with His plan for our life.

Second, asking God for guidance exposes doors we would not have noticed or given much thought to. He always has bigger plans than we do, and following His guidance can result in fulfillment, opportunity, and rewards that we never would have imagined.

Finally, asking God for guidance cultivates a strong sense of dependency and trust in Him. We come to rely more on His direction than on our own finite comprehension. As a result, our relationship with Him is strengthened and He is able to work powerfully in and through us.

Thus, rather than taking pride in our knowledge, let's humble ourselves and seek God's guidance in all that we do. By doing this, we shall reap the abundant rewards of His direction, discernment, and favor.

BREAKING FREE FROM DESTRUCTIVE PATTERNS

"Do not conform to the pattern of this world but be transformed by the renewing of your mind." - Romans 12:2 (NIV)

We all suffer with our share of poor habits as men of God. Addictions, harmful mental patterns, and poisonous behavior are a few examples of these habits. However, we are not expected to follow the ways of this world. God desires for us to have transformed lives through mental renewal in accordance with His Word.

It takes intentionality and faith in God's power to overcome unhealthy behaviors. We can't depend on our own might to break these habits. Rather, we have to surrender to God's direction and let His Spirit change us from the inside out.

Let us acknowledge our negative habits and ask God to help us break them as we move closer to freedom today. Allowing Him to regenerate our thoughts and transform our actions, let's give Him our will and desires. We shall find the fortitude and encouragement we require in His presence to overcome harmful habits.

Recall that change is a process and might not occur immediately. However, we can truly break free from our negative habits by regularly surrendering to God's transformative power. Let us put our faith in His constancy, confident that He will give us the courage and direction we require to overcome our limitations and live the abundant life He desires for us.

ACCEPTING YOUR LIFE'S PURPOSE AS GOD'S

Jeremiah 29:11 - "For I know the plans I have for you," declares the LORD, "plans to prosper you and not to harm you, plans to give you hope and a future."

Men frequently wonder what their life's purpose and direction are. It's possible for us to feel disoriented, uneasy, or overburdened by the choices and obligations that confront us. It's critical to keep in mind that God has a purpose for each of us during these uncertain times.

God communicates to His people directly in Jeremiah 29:11, telling them that He has plans for their lives. Plans to provide them with a future, prosperity, and hope. This verse serves as a reminder that God is actively involved in guiding and shaping our path and that we are not alone on this journey.

It takes trust and surrender to acknowledge God's purpose for our lives. It entails admitting that although God's methods are higher and His knowledge greater than ours, His intentions may not always line up with our own preferences or expectations. It entails accepting the special abilities, interests, and gifts that God has given each of us and putting them to good use for His glory.

Accepting that God is the one who created our life's purpose allows us to live in peace and satisfaction because we know that we are right where He wants us to be. We can have faith that He will provide us with whatever we require to carry out His purposes for our life. Let's submit to His will, ask for His direction, and bravely pursue the goals He has for us.

DISCOVERING HAPPINESS IN GOD'S WORK

"Commit your work to the Lord, and your plans will be established." - Proverbs 16:3

It is easy to overlook the genuine source of happiness in a world where people are continuously seeking satisfaction through worldly accomplishments, success, and material goods. However, as men of faith, we have the honor of realizing a more profound and satisfying happiness—happiness that arises from giving our labor to the Lord.

Proverbs 16:3 serves as a helpful reminder of the significance of giving God the credit for our labor. We set ourselves up for success when we submit to

His will, seek His direction, and acknowledge His sovereignty. When we give our plans to God, He pledges to carry them out.

Giving God our aspirations, anxieties, and wishes is the first step toward finding contentment in His work. It entails looking for His will for our life and trying to glorify Him in whatever we do. We can find happiness and fulfillment in our job that transcends all material achievement when we include God into it.

Let's pause today to consider the job we have done. Do we sincerely intend to pursue God's will and guidance in our careers? Are we ready to give up our plans and be receptive to His guidance? May we, as we go about our everyday business, find the real joy that comes from coordinating our efforts with God's perfect will.

OVERCOMING UNCERTAINTY WITH GOD'S VALIDATION

"Blessed is the man who trusts in the Lord,
whose trust is the Lord." - Jeremiah 17:7 (ESV)

We all have periods of uncertainty and doubt in our life. We might doubt our intentions, choices, and skills. It is essential to ask God for confirmation during those times. Our Heavenly Father's unconditional love and acceptance define our identity and worth, not any earthly norm.

When we trust God, we put all our trust in Him, even when we don't know where to go. He promises to be with us and to lead us when we put our trust in

Him. His validation is greater than any human endorsement or material achievement.

To overcome uncertainty, we must surrender our fears and worries to God, knowing that He is in control. Through prayer, reading God's Word, and getting sage advice from other believers, we can look for His confirmation. God will give us the confirmation we require in His perfect time so that we can go forward confident in the knowledge that He has a purpose for our lives.

Today, let us trust in the Lord wholeheartedly, allowing His validation to outweigh any uncertainties we may face. Recall that we put our faith in the omnipotent and dependable God who goes before us, not in our own might or competence.

THE INFLUENCE OF MOTIVATION

"Blessed is the one who does not walk in step with the wicked or stand in the way that sinners take or sit in the company of mockers, but whose delight is in the law of the Lord, and who meditates on his Law Day and night." - Psalm 1:1-2 (NIV)

It's important to consider our reasons when we make decisions in our spiritual journey. Our decisions and, in the end, our character are shaped by our motivations. It is simple to lose focus on the important things in life in a world full of temptations and diversions.

The passage from Psalm 1 serves as a reminder that when we align our motives with God's truth, true rewards follow. We are to delight in and think about the law of the Lord Day and night, not to be swayed by the ways of the world. This entails asking for His insight and direction before making any decisions.

Our desires are less likely to be misguided by evil influences or fall into the pitfalls of when they are based in God's Word.

Let's consider our motivations for today. Are they founded in the truth of God and directed by His Word? Let us endeavor to harmonize our choices and aspirations with His will, letting His influence mold our personalities. May we be a light to others in this world, guiding them to our heavenly father's love and grace.

PRIDE OVERCOMES THROUGH HUMILITY

Proverbs 16:18 (ESV)
"Pride goes before destruction, and a haughty spirit before a fall."

In the modern world, pride is a prevalent characteristic that frequently leads individuals down a destructive road. It is simple to be caught up in the trap of overestimating our own talents, accomplishments, and capabilities. But the Bible forewarns us that arrogance precedes fall and pride comes before ruin.

Men who want to live lives committed to God need to be careful to keep pride out of their hearts.

Being humble is the key that opens the door to getting over our pride. It is an admission that God is the source of all that we own and who we are.

We confess our need for God's wisdom and direction in our life when we humble ourselves before Him. We acknowledge that our accomplishments are a product of God's grace and favor bestowed upon us, rather than being entirely our own.

Let's pray to God, asking for His guidance and giving Him control over our goals and objectives, to conquer pride. Let us be receptive to guidance, advice, and correction from those we can trust. By doing this, we may grow truly and stay away from the negative effects of pride.

Let us try to walk in humility today, depending only on God's might and grace. We may overcome the damaging effects of pride by acknowledging our need for Him and humbling ourselves. May humility be a defining characteristic of our life, bringing us closer to God and having a bigger influence on the world.

DISCOVERING HAPPINESS IN GOD'S WORK

"Commit your work to the Lord, and your plans will be established." - Proverbs 16:3 (ESV)

It's simple to lose sight of what genuinely offers joy and contentment in a culture where financial riches and worldly achievement are frequently associated with happiness. We are called to find satisfaction in carrying out God's will in our life as men of God.

This Proverbs passage serves as a helpful reminder of the significance of giving our labor to the Lord. It inspires us to ask for His direction and conform our goals to His will. God promises to make our plans when we put our faith in Him and give Him control over our actions.

The first step to finding enjoyment in God's work is to look for His plan for our life. It's about finding fulfillment and purpose in carrying out the duties and obligations He has given us, such as being a devoted spouse, a a devoted worker, a loving father, or a devoted member of our church and community.

We feel a profound feeling of contentment and satisfaction when we put God's service ahead of our own goals and wants. Our labor takes on the role of a worship tool, a chance to show people the kindness and love of God.

Let us give our job to the Lord today, relying on His supply and seeking His direction. When we do this, we will find genuine delight in realizing His plan for our life. May God make our plans and pour down His glorious benefits on our labor.

THE BLESSING OF TRUE FRIENDSHIP

Proverbs 17:17 - "A friend loves at all times, and a
brother is born for a time of adversity."

God has given us friendship as a priceless gift.
Genuine companions are individuals that accompany
us during life's highs and lows, providing affection,
assistance, and motivation. Sincere friendships are
uncommon in a society that frequently prizes
superficial relationships, and they need to be
treasured.

This poem serves as a reminder of the benefits
that come from genuine friendship. Someone who
loves us without conditions, irrespective of our
previous transgressions or current circumstances, is

a real friend. They offer a sympathetic ear, a consoling shoulder, and sage advice, supporting us both in happy and sad times.

But genuine friendship is based on more than simply receiving; it also involves giving. We are expected to love our friends unconditionally, just as they love us. When they are going through hardship, we must be ready to lend them our time, prayers, and support.

Think for a moment about the friendships you have. Are they firmly based on an unwavering base of love and support? Are you prepared to give of yourself, even under trying circumstances, as a loyal friend? Recall that God is the epitome of what real friendship looks like. He invites us to show others the same love that He has always shown us. May we endeavor to nurture and cherish the favor of genuine companionship in our existence.

ESTABLISHING A FIRM BASIS IN CHRIST

"Therefore, everyone who hears these words of mine and puts them into practice is like a wise man who built his house on the rock." - Matthew 7:24

It is imperative that we develop a solid foundation in Christ as men of faith. Our lives need a firm basis in the teachings of Jesus, just as a home requires a strong foundation. This means hearing what He has to say, but also acting upon it.

It is simple for us to veer off the straight and narrow in a world full of temptations and diversion. But when we base our lives on the unwavering truth of God's Word, we are strong enough to weather life's storms. We have the capacity to make morally sound choices that are in line with His desire.

Having a solid foundation in Christ also entails asking for His direction in every area of our lives. It serves as a reminder to give Him control over our own goals and objectives so that He can guide us. By doing this, we give ourselves the opportunity to enjoy the many blessings and sense of fulfillment that result from abiding by His Word.

Let us, as men of faith, make a commitment to erecting our lives upon the unwavering foundation of Jesus. May we actively put His teachings into practice in addition to just hearing them. By doing this, we shall walk in accordance with His will and feel the power, knowledge, and purpose that accompany it.

RELYING ON GOD'S FAITHFULNESS IN RELATIONSHIPS

Proverbs 3:5-6 - "Trust in the Lord with all your heart and lean not on your own understanding; in all your ways submit to him, and he will make your paths straight."

Whether it's with friends, family, or love partners, we frequently find ourselves depending on our own knowledge and insight in our interactions. We attempt to exert control over the situation and make things go as we had planned. But God's Word serves as a constant reminder that genuine relationship success and joy only result from complete confidence in Him.

Relying too much on our own knowledge confines our interactions to our own viewpoints, experiences, and prejudices. Fear, resentment from the past, or self-interest may influence our decisions. However, when we give God control over our relationships, we ask Him to lead us in all of our choices, interactions, and deeds.

Recognizing that God understands what is best for us and our relationships is the first step toward trusting in His faithfulness. It entails giving our goals and aspirations over to His tender direction. He promises to straighten our paths as we trust on Him, pointing us in the direction of happy, meaningful, and God-honoring relationships.

Let us pause now and renew our commitment to God in our relationships. Let us put our faith in His trustworthiness and ask for His discernment and direction in everything that we do. Knowing that when we rely on Him, we may achieve genuine joy and success, may our relationships be characterized by His love, grace, and truth.

MANAGING DISAPPOINTMENT WITH HOPE

Romans 8:28 – "And we know that in all things God works for the good of those who love him, who have been called according to his purpose."

There are highs and lows in life, and disappointment is an unwelcome but necessary aspect of being human. But hope is a wonderful weapon that men of religion must help us deal with disappointment. Romans 8:28 tells us that even in the face of adversity, God is constantly working for our benefit.

Disappointment can cause sresentment, irritation, and even hopelessness. However, we may find hope in the knowledge that God has a purpose for everything when we firmly plant our hearts in the truth of God's Word. Recalling that our heavenly Father is sovereign and that everything is working for our ultimate benefit will help us when we are disappointed.

We are commanded, as men of faith, to have faith in God's plan even in the face of uncertainty or deviation from our expectations. The knowledge that God is use our disappointments to mold, polish, and eventually bring us closer to Himself gives us comfort.

Therefore, let's not give up hope when disappointment knocks on our door. Rather, let us cling to the assurance found in Romans 8:28, knowing that God is obediently constructing a lovely and redeeming narrative in our life behind the scenes. May we be able to endure any setback with unwavering confidence in Him and hope in His kindness and constancy.

THE POWER OF YOUR WORDS

Proverbs 18:21 (NIV) - "The tongue has the power of life and death, and those who love it will eat its fruit."

Have you ever given your words any thought as to how they affect those around you? Our words have great power; they may destroy and inflict suffering, or they can provide life and healing. Proverbs 18:21 states that our tongues have the capacity to both bring forth life and death. This poem serves as a reminder of the responsibility and weight we bear when we speak.

Our words have the power to mold our relationships, affect our own feelings and ideas, and even determine our own fate. Our words have the power to either uplift or depress other people. Have you ever made a statement that you subsequently regretted? Everyone has. Although it might be simple to allow our feelings control what we say, as adherents of Christ, we are called to a higher standard.

Speaking words that bring life reflects God's heart. He used words to create the world, and He wants us to use words to encourage, uplift, and give life to others. But it's equally critical to acknowledge the influence of our negative language. They have the capacity to hurt and create long-lasting harm.

Let's be aware of the impact that our words can have on other people. Decide to express love, affirmation, encouragement, and hope via your words. Seek God's direction as you speak, letting the Holy Spirit impart wisdom and grace to your words. As you do, you'll see firsthand the positive impact your words can have on others around you.

GIVING UP CONTROL TO GOD

"Blessed are those who trust in the LORD, whose trust is the LORD." - Jeremiah 17:7

Surrendering to God's designs for our life can be tough in a society that prizes independence and power. We frequently catch ourselves stressing, attempting to solve problems on our own, and straining. But only when we relinquish control and put our faith in the Lord can we experience genuine contentment and serenity.

Jeremiah tells us that blessings come to those who rely on the Lord. By putting our faith in God, we confess that He is in control and that His purposes are higher than our own. To give Him our goals, dreams, and anxieties demands humility.

Giving our worries and anxieties over to God also entails giving up control. We can be released from the weight of our burdens when we put our confidence in His direction and provision. Knowing that He is in charge and will always guide us in the correct direction gives us peace.

Let us choose to consciously cede authority to God today. Let us put all our faith and confidence in Him, knowing that He is dependable and will keep His word. We may enjoy His benefits, serenity, and happiness in our life as we submit to His designs.

GETTING THROUGH TEMPTATION
WITH GOD'S WORD

Bible Verse: Psalm 119:11 - "I have hidden your word in my heart that I might not sin against you."

It might be difficult to stay on the straight road and make decisions that glorify God in a world full with distractions and temptations. We are not, however, left to battle these temptations on our own. God has kindly provided us with His Word to lead and guard us.

The psalmist recognized the effectiveness of God's Word in warding off temptation. He realized that it was crucial to internalize God's Word rather than just reading it. Knowing God's Word only academically is insufficient; we also need to absorb it and let it change our thoughts and feelings.

We may rely on the truth provided in God's Word when we are tempted. His assurances, directives, and admonitions function as a guide through the obstacles and allures we face. Scripture memorization and meditation provide us the power to overcome temptation and make informed decisions.

Additionally, the Bible gives us examples of people who resisted temptation. Their experiences give us insightful insights and motivate us to imitate them. We can find support, vigor, and direction in God's Word to withstand temptation and lead lives that glorify Him.

Let us make a commitment to keep God's Word hidden in our hearts, to get to know it well, and to rely on its wisdom and truth to help us resist temptation. His Word becomes a shield as we ingrain it into our consciousness, guiding us away from the perils of sin and toward a life that pleases God.

LEADING A PURPOSEFUL LIFE

Proverbs 3:6 - "In all your ways acknowledge him,
and he will make your paths straight."

Men frequently ask themselves what their life's purpose is. We try to set a good example for others around us and to lead by example. However, there are moments when we get disoriented and overwhelmed by the options and obligations in front of us.

Proverbs 3:6 reminds us that praising God in whatever we do is essential to living a life with meaning. He pledges to straighten our paths when we ask for His counsel and insight. This implies that He will lead us along the correct route toward our actual purpose as we align our lives with His will and give Him control over our goals.

To acknowledge God in all that we do is to be humble and open to receiving. It entails seeking His will before deciding, talking to Him in prayer, and allowing Him to guide our hearts. By doing this, we may put our confidence in Him to guide us toward a meaningful and impactful existence.

Let's make a commitment to thanking God in every aspect of our lives starting today. Let's ask Him for direction and give Him control over our plans. As we do, we may have faith that He will guide us toward living a life that serves Him and reward our efforts to do good.

OVERCOMING FEAR WITH GOD'S STRENGTH

"For God has not given us a spirit of fear, but of power and of love and of a sound mind." - 2 Timothy 1:7

Everybody experiences fear at some time in their life. Our fears can prevent us from living the full lives that God has intended for us, whether they be fears of success, rejection, or the unknown. However, we are not called to live in dread as men of faith.

God has not given us a spirit of fear, but of power, love, and sound mind, as 2 Timothy 1:7 reminds us. God's strength is available to us, so we may conquer any fear that may arise.

We may access a reservoir of strength that surpasses any fear we may encounter when we rely on God's might. Fear is no longer able to control us when we genuinely understand God's unchanging love for us. And we may face every circumstance with confidence and intelligence because God has given us good minds.

Let us keep in mind today that fear has no place in our lives. Let us look to God in times of fear and find strength in His might, love, and sound mind. With God at our side, we can conquer any fear that tries to prevent us from moving forward and confidently pursue the goals and plans He has for us.

RESTING IN GOD'S PRESENCE

Bible Verse: Psalm 46:10 - "Be still, and know that I am God."

It's simple to overlook the value of just taking a break and spending time in God's presence amid life's hustle and bustle. Distractions, obligations, and difficulties abound in our lives, sometimes leaving us feeling depleted and worn out. But God invites us to set aside time on purpose to be still and acknowledge His divinity.

We give our cares and anxieties over to God's skilled hands when we lie down in His presence. We admit that He is in charge and that we are not. We are reminded of God's strength, fidelity, and undying love for us amid the silence.

Perspective is another benefit of resting in God's presence. It enables us to realign with His will and put our attention back on what really matters. We allow our hearts to be open to receiving His direction, solace, and serenity when we set aside time to be still before Him.

Let's intentionally work to create times of silence in our lives today. Let us take a moment to stop and relax in God's presence among our hectic schedules. Give Him permission to uplift our souls, renew our spirits, and deepen our faith. As we keep in mind that He is God and that He is in charge, may we find comfort and tranquility.

THE BLESSING OF GOD'S MERCY

Psalm 103:11, "For as high as the heavens are above the earth, so great is his mercy toward those who fear him."

We are all fallible and fall short of God's ideal standards in life. We frequently find ourselves in need of His forgiveness and kindness. But the lovely thing is that we may easily access God's kindness. It is a gift that is freely provided; we do not need to earn it or deserve it.

Men sometimes find it difficult to own up to their shortcomings and ask for assistance. But we enter a realm of rewards when we humble ourselves before the Lord and confess our need for His compassion.

We become free of shame and guilt when we accept God's kindness. We are offered the opportunity to walk in God's forgiveness and a new beginning. We are enabled to show grace, forgive others, and radiate His love to those around us by His mercy.

Let us rejoice in the kindness of God today. May we come to Him in humility, confessing our transgressions, and relying only on His grace. Recall that His mercy is boundless in love and extends to us the opportunity to begin again, regardless of our transgressions.

Give this scripture some thought, and then ask the Lord to show you His kindness in your life. Give yourself over to His forgiveness, and He will heal your heart and make you into the man He created you to be. In your path of faith, be open to the amazing rewards that result from accepting God's kindness.

FORTIFYING FAITH IN TOUGH TIMES

"So we fix our eyes not on what is seen, but on what is unseen, since what is seen is temporary, but what is unseen is eternal." - 2 Corinthians 4:18

We frequently encounter tough and trying circumstances in life, which can cause us to lose faith and feel powerless. But even in the face of adversity, it is our duty as Christians to strengthen our confidence in God. The secret is to change our viewpoint from the visible to the invisible.

It's normal to concentrate on our current situation and whatever suffering we may be going through when things are unpleasant. However, this passage serves as a reminder that although the things

116

we can see are fleeting, the things that are unseen and everlasting are more important.

Focusing on the invisible allows us to put our faith and hope in God's enduring love and unfulfilled promises. Adversity is the place where our faith is put to the test and grown stronger. We are reminded that we should not rely just on our own might but also on God's trustworthiness.

Recall that adversity is supposed to shape us into better people, not to destroy us. Our confidence in God grows unwavering as we rely on His constancy and His sovereignty. Let us strengthen our trust today in the knowledge that God is always at our side and is working everything out for our benefit, even when circumstances are difficult.

DEVELOPING A HEART OF COMPASSION

Ephesians 4:32 - "Be kind and compassionate to one another, forgiving each other, just as in Christ God forgave you."

In a society that prioritizes accomplishment, prosperity, and self-interest, it is simple to undervalue the significance of cultivating empathy. Nonetheless, we are obligated to emulate Christ's compassion and love for others as His disciples.

More than merely having sympathy for someone, compassion is an empathetic sreaction that aims to lessen their pain. Our hearts become receptive to the needs and challenges of others around us as we

118

cultivate compassion. It demands that we put other people's needs and wants aside in order to prioritize their welfare.

We must first acknowledge the extent of God's concern for us before we can begin to grow a compassionate heart. Consider the grace and pardon He has bestowed upon you via Christ. We may then provide compassion to others because of this abundance of love and grace.

Today let us to treat everyone we come into contact with love and compassion today. Spend some time understanding, supporting, and listening to people who are in pain. In addition to having an influence on other people's lives, when we emulate Christ's compassion, we also open the door for God to use ourselves as a vehicle for change and healing.

EMBRACING GOD'S UNCONDITIONAL LOVE IN DIVERSITY

"Accept one another, then, just as Christ accepted you, in order to bring praise to God." - Romans 15:7

God's love provides us with a wonderful chance to accept variety and create bridges of togetherness in a world where differences frequently cause us to part. It is vital for us to comprehend and accept one another as men of faith, just as Christ has received us.

Gazing around us, we behold a mosaic of distinct persons, every one with their own narratives, histories, and life encounters. God's love is limitless and unaffected by our differences. He exhorts us to love without conditions and to imitate Him.

By showing acceptance to others, we honor God and show the world how much He loves us. Our variety unites us in a way that amply demonstrates His capacity for transformation.

It is a challenge for men of faith to see past preconceptions and biases and recognize the intrinsic worth and value in every person in a culture that frequently promotes divisiveness. We should make an effort to welcome, appreciate, and accept the variety that exists around us since God's love is most evident when it comes to our differences.

PUTTING YOUR TRUST IN GOD'S CAREER PLAN

Proverbs 3:5-6 "Trust in the LORD with all your heart and lean not on your own understanding; in all your ways submit to him, and he will make your paths straight."

In the fast-paced, cutthroat world of today, worrying about our future goals and professions is a common occurrence. In an attempt to make the best decisions that would lead to success and contentment, we might discover that we are continuously challenging and gaining understanding of ourselves. But the Word of God presents an other viewpoint. It inspires us to place all of our faith in Him and yield our own understanding and goals to His direction.

Recognizing that God is more familiar with us than we are requires us to trust Him with our jobs. He is aware of our wants, shortcomings, and talents. We ask Him to direct our steps and match our pathways with His perfect will when we give Him our plans.

This passage serves as a reminder that God cares about all of our everyday activities, including our occupations, in addition to our spiritual life. We enable God to reveal His divine purpose for us when we fully trust Him and set aside our own understanding. He assures us that he will straighten our routes and bring us to the greatest connections, growth, and opportunity.

Faith and submission are necessary when we put our confidence in God's professional plan. It entails asking for His direction in prayer and sage advice from godly role models. It also entails remaining receptive to His guidance, even when it forces us to step outside of our comfort zones.

THE POWER OF UNCEASING PRAYER

"Rejoice in hope; be patient in affliction; be persistent in prayer." - Romans 12:12

We are not unfamiliar with the power of prayer as men of faith. We may directly communicate with God via prayer, asking for His wisdom, strength, and direction in every area of life. However, how often do we actually accept the effectiveness of constant prayer?

We are urged to pray consistently in Romans 12:12. This entails persistently seeking God's presence in happy and hopeful moments as well as in difficult ones. Through prayer, we may stay in close contact with God and allow Him to perform powerful work in our lives.

Men deal with difficulties, temptations, and problems daily. That's when persistent prayer turns into our most powerful tool. By keeping our hearts in line with God's desire, prayer fortifies our determination to withstand temptation and make morally sound choices.

Let's commit to constant prayer and take this verse to heart. Let us develop a prayerful way of living, one that rejoices in hope, endures suffering patiently, and never gives up on seeking God's presence. We may access the boundless power of our heavenly Father and witness His life-changing action through persistent prayer.

FINDING SATISFACTION IN GOD'S PROVIDENCE

"Trust in the Lord with all your heart, and do not lean on your own understanding. In all your ways acknowledge him, and he will make straight your paths." - Proverbs 3:5-6 (ESV)

It is simple to fall into the trap of looking to material belongings for fulfillment in a culture where quick pleasure and the persistent chase of them are the norm. Because we think that achieving success, money, and fame would make us truly happy, we yearn for them. But only in God's providence can one find genuine satisfaction.

The thoughtful and loving provision that God makes for every part of our life is known as providence. It includes His direction, defense, and supply. His ideal design for us can satisfy us when we put our faith in Him and recognize Him in everything.

It takes a change of perspective to find contentment in God's providence. We have to rely on God's knowledge and let go of our own understanding. This entails submitting our goals and intentions to His will, even when it differs from our own.

We may live in peace knowing that God is bringing everything together for our benefit when we put our faith in His providence. Even when His time and ways don't match our own expectations, we may still find happiness in them. We can achieve genuine contentment via relying in Him, surpassing the fleeting delights of this life, and rest in His provision.

Therefore, let us always look for God's providence in our lives. With complete confidence that He is dependable and will straighten our pathways, let's put all of our trust in Him. May His ideal design bring us real happiness, and may His supply fill our hearts to overflowing thanksgiving and contentment.

LIVING WITH GOD'S TRUST

"Trust in the Lord with all your heart, and do not lean on your own understanding. In all your ways acknowledge him, and he will make straight your paths." - Proverbs 3:5-6

It is simple to get weary of faith in God in this uncertain and difficult world. We could doubt His intentions or wonder why specific events occur in our lives. But as Christians, we are expected to live with God's confidence at the center of our being.

Giving up our own understanding is a prerequisite for trusting in the Lord. It entails admitting that He has a better plan for our life than we do and that His methods are higher than ours.

Knowing that our Heavenly Father is in control may bring us peace even in situations that seem overwhelming.

Seeking God's counsel in all areas of our lives is a sign that we are living in His trust. It entails incorporating Him into the process of making decisions and letting His discernment influence our decisions. We may expect Him to straighten our pathways when we recognize Him in all of our actions. He will lead us toward His plan for our life by guiding and directing our steps.

Let us make the decision to base our lives on God's trust today. Let's put all our trust in Him and let go of our worries and anxieties. May the knowledge that He is trustworthy and that His intentions for us are good bring us comfort. Our confidence, joy, and a meaningful existence in His presence will come from trusting in the Lord.

THE SIGNIFICANCE OF HAVING A GRATEFUL HEART

1 Thessalonians 5:18 - "Give thanks in all circumstances; for this is God's will for you in Christ Jesus."

It's simple to become overwhelmed and lose sight of the blessings all around us in the fast-paced, chaotic world of today. But even in the midst of turmoil, it is our duty as men of religion to be grateful. Being thankful is more than just saying "thank you" when things are going well; it also entails looking for opportunities to express gratitude in every situation.

Having gratitude in our hearts causes us to realize the gifts that we frequently take for granted.

It reminds us of God's faithfulness and provision, bringing us serenity and satisfaction. Having gratitude in our hearts helps us to remain calm throughout chaotic times..

Recall that even in the most trying circumstances, there are benefits to be found. A thankful heart is powerful because it may always serve as a reminder of God's goodness and presence. Therefore, let us practice everyday expression of appreciation from the heart, as it brings God's serenity into our life and helps us to align with His plan.

Reflect: Give the previous week some thought. Are there any events or circumstances for which you have the option to express gratitude? How do you learn to be thankful despite the craziness in your day-to-day existence?

Make a conscious effort to locate five things for which you are thankful today. Put them in writing and give God thanks for each one. By doing this, you open your heart to receive God's serenity and tranquility even in the middle of chaos.

RENEWED STRENGTH: FINDING DAILY INSPIRATION IN GOD'S WORD

Isaiah 40:31 - "But those who hope in the LORD will renew their strength. They will soar on wings like eagles; they will run and not grow weary; they will walk and not be faint."

Life frequently saps our vitality and leaves us exhausted and drained. We might not have the energy to carry on due to the pressures of our jobs, relationships, or other commitments. God's Word may provide us with solace and rejuvenation during these times.

Isaiah 40:31 serves as a reminder that the Lord will replenish our strength when we place our faith and confidence in Him. God can give us the strength and stamina to finish our race without tiring and to face life's obstacles head-on, just like an eagle soars over the skies.

Establish the practice of spending time in God's Word each day to receive renewed inspiration and strength. Your spirit will be renewed by his lessons and promises, and you will have the strength to handle any circumstance. Give yourself over to the Holy Spirit's encouraging and hopeful words.

Therefore, keep in mind that God is the source of new strength no matter what you may be going through today. Come to Him, put your faith in His promises, and draw encouragement from His Word. You will then have the enthusiasm and vigor to face life's obstacles and live in His bountiful grace.

RESTORING THE MIND: BUILDING STRENGTH IN GOD'S WORD

Psalm 119:28, the psalmist declares, "My soul is weary with sorrow; strengthen me according to your word."

Distractions, disputes, and demands abound in our environment, which quickly weakens our resolve and wears out our thoughts. It is imperative that, as men of faith, we use the power of God's Word to strengthen and repair our brains.

We must consciously set aside time each day to read and concentrate on Scripture if we are to rebuild our brains and strengthen our faith in God's Word. By doing this, we start to bring our thinking into line

134

with God's realities, which helps us gain perspective and discover new inspiration for the difficulties we encounter.

We pause to consider how you are feeling mentally. Do you feel worn out and overburdened? Think about making reading and reflecting on God's Word a regular habit. Let His lessons and promises to bolster and direct your thoughts. Keep in mind that you will discover restored hope, serenity, and the solid foundation upon which to build your life as you strengthen yourself in God's Word.

STRENGTHENING MARRIAGES THROUGH GOD'S LOVE

Isaiah 40:31, "But those who hope in the Lord will renew their strength. They will soar on wings like eagles; they will run and not grow weary, they will walk and not be faint."

Men often have a lot of obligations and obstacles in their life. Demands at work and obligations to one's family may quickly leave one feeling worn out and stressed. However, the Word of God is a tremendous source of inspiration and power available to us as followers of Christ.

Through consistent reading of God's Word and reflection on His promises, we can be regenerated, encouraged, and guided. The important thing is to regularly interact with God's Word, whether that means memorizing passages, reading a chapter of the Bible every day, or joining a Bible study group.

Our marriages may be revolutionized as we look to God's Word for guidance and support. Through the application of Christian values such as selflessness, forgiveness, and love, we may experience God's love fully and fortify our marriages.

Let's make a commitment to putting God first and relying on His guidance and strength every day. We may get the motivation and direction we need to foster love, trust, and respect in our marriages from His Word. May our unions serve as an example of God's love and His glory to the rest of the world.

DEVELOPING GODLY CHARACTER IN YOUR CHILDREN

Psalm 119:105 tells us, "Your word is a lamp to my feet and a light to my path."

We all experience fatigue and weariness when faced with obstacles in life. We could wonder if our efforts are worthwhile and what our goal is. When we are feeling tired, we can go to God's Word for inspiration and new strength.

It is vital for us to value spending time in God's Word as men of faith. The Bible is filled with tales of common individuals who shown great faith. By seeing them, we can develop understanding of how God can act in and through us.

Whatever our situation, there is clarity and purpose when we live according to God's Word. The Scriptures provide us the bravery and fortitude we require to firmly maintain our faith.

Think for a moment about how often you interact with God's Word. Do you schedule daily reading and meditation time on His truth? Do you let His Word guide your decisions, thoughts, and deeds?

Decide to give God's Word top priority in your life. Allocate a dedicated period of time every day for reading a section or studying a certain Bible book. Ask God to strengthen you and give you the confidence and discernment to steadfastly maintain your faith while you spend time in His Word.

Let us never forget that the Bible is our source of strength and inspiration. May it lead us in life and give us the courage to uphold our convictions, even in the face of adversity.

BUILDING STRONG CHARACTER IN A MODERN WORLD

"Do not conform to the pattern of this world but be transformed by the renewing of your mind. Then you will be able to test and approve what God's will is—his good, pleasing and perfect will." - Romans 12:2

It might be challenging to live a strong character in a world that frequently contradicts our morals and ideologies. We are constantly faced with temptations and diversions in the modern world, which may quickly cause us to lose sight of what really important. But as men of God, we have an obligation to overcome these effects and develop a solid moral code that demonstrates the life-changing power of Jesus.

Romans 12:2 exhorts us to renew our thoughts rather than follow the ways of this world. To be changed is to align oneself with God's truth and purpose for our life by altering our thoughts and behaviors. It necessitates that we reject the impulse to act in accordance with cultural standards that run counter to our principles and instead God's will.

Our ideas are the first step in developing strong character. God's Word must be ingrained in our thoughts and we must protect them from harmful influences. Renewing our brains and changing us from the inside out is made possible by regularly immersing ourselves in scripture and seeking the Lord's guidance.

We may identify and embrace God's intention for our life as we develop strong character via our refreshed thinking. By doing this, we become resilient against the difficulties the contemporary world throws at us and shine a light on God's love and truth for people around us.

May we always strive to build strong character in a world that desperately needs godly men of integrity, guided by Romans 12:2, and transformed by the renewing of our minds.

GIVING UP TO THE WISDOM OF GOD

."Trust in the LORD with all your heart and lean not on your own understanding." - Proverbs 3:5

Life will inevitably include change. Circumstances and events are subject to change and evolution, much like the seasons. Change may occasionally seem unsettling, terrifying, and overpowering. It is in these moments that we must put all of our faith in God.

In all of His knowledge, God is aware of every turn and turn that awaits us. He looks beyond the boundaries of our comprehension and grasps the greater scheme of things. By putting our faith in Him, we give our worries and anxieties into His capable care.

It is necessary for us to give up our dependence on our own understanding to fully trust God. It entails realizing that He has all the answers, and we don't. It serves as a continual reminder that God is faithfully leading our feet, especially in situations when the route ahead appears uncertain.

Let us rely on the stability of God's character and promises throughout these times of change. May the knowledge that He is our constant companion and that He is guiding us towards His perfect plan give us comfort as we navigate these uncharted waters. We may confront change with bravery and confidence if we have steadfast trust in Him, knowing that He is in charge.

FEAR ABOUT THE FUTURES

Do not be anxious about anything, but in every situation, by prayer and petition, with thanksgiving, present your requests to God." - Philippians 4:6

Fear, especially when focused on the future, can often paralyze and hinder us from living a fulfilled life. It is natural to have concerns and uncertainties about what lies ahead, but as men of faith, we are called to surrender those fears to God.

In the Bible, we are repeatedly reminded not to be anxious, and this verse from Philippians reminds us that we have a loving and caring God who is always ready to listen to our concerns. Instead of allowing fear to consume us, we are encouraged to turn to prayer and present our requests, worries, and desires to God.

Surrendering our fears about the future is an act of faith and trust in God's plan for our lives. It is a declaration that we believe in His goodness, wisdom, and sovereignty. As we release our worries and place them in God's hands, we can experience a profound sense of peace and assurance.

Let us remember that surrendering our fears is not a one-time event but a continuous process. It requires daily surrendering and entrusting our lives and future into God's loving care. In doing so, we can live with confidence, knowing that He will guide and provide for us every step of the way.

THE STRENGTH OF GOD'S COMFORT

"He gives power to the weak and strength to the powerless." - Isaiah 40:29 (NLT)

Where can we get strength when we are helpless and weak? The consoling presence of God holds the solution. The difficulties we face in life might leave us feeling exhausted, overburdened, and unable to handle the difficulties that lie ahead. However, God promises to give the weak people strength and the helpless people power.

This phrase serves as a reminder that genuine power comes from God alone. As men, we frequently attempt to depend on our own strength and ability to overcome challenges. He is the source of boundless

146

strength and consolation, ready to give us confidence when we feel unworthy and helpless.

God urges us to come to Him in prayer during our trials. We may communicate with the All-Powerful Creator via prayer, and He is always willing to hear from us and give us the strength we require. He pledges to give us the strength to endure, the bravery to face hardship, and the discernment to get us through challenging times.

May we never forget that we are not alone when we feel helpless. God's consoling presence is all around us, providing us with the daily strength we require. Let us rely on Him, put our faith in His word, and let His power see us through all of life's obstacles.

OVERCOMING COMPARISON THROUGH GOD'S AFFIRMATION

"For am I now seeking the approval of man, or of God? Or am I trying to please man? If I were still trying to please man, I would not be a servant of Christ." - Galatians 1:10 (ESV)

It is vital for us as men to seek God's affirmation instead of other people's acceptance in a culture that often tempts us to compare ourselves to others. We are reminded of this fact by the apostle Paul in his epistle to the Galatians.

We might look to those around us for approval and recognition when we let ourselves get caught up in the trap of comparing ourselves to others. Paul, nevertheless, asks us to consider our motivations: Are we trying to appease God or the public? Are we attempting to get other people's acceptance and approval to satisfy ourselves?

Serving man pleases no longer constitutes serving Christ. God invites us to live not for other people's acceptance or recognition but for His glory. He alone is the source of our identity and worth; other people's ideas are not.

To overcome comparison, we must change our perspective and turn to God for validation. He reminds us of our worth and purpose in Him, affirming us as His treasured children. We can be released from the slavery of comparison and live as Christ's followers by focusing on God's affirmation rather than the ephemeral praise of people.

THE BLESSING OF GOD'S JOY IN TRIALS

"The Lord Himself goes before you and will be with you; He will never leave you nor forsake you. Do not be afraid; do not be discouraged." - Deuteronomy 31:8 (NIV)

There will always be difficulties and obstacles in life that we must overcome. While some challenges can appear overwhelming, others might be minor. However, because we are men of faith, we may take solace in the knowledge that God is happy despite all of our difficulties.

The scripture above serves as a reminder that the Lord goes before us, guiding us and laying the groundwork for our future. He pledges to always walk with us, never abandoning us. This strong reassurance ought to give us the courage to overcome every obstacle that we encounter.

Fear and despair brought on by trials might make us doubt God's existence and our own talents. But the Bible instructs us to put our confidence in God and not be terrified. He is our ever-present source of insight, consolation, and strength.

The knowledge that these challenges may build our character, increase our faith, and bring us closer to God is the benefit of God's delight in tribulations. They provide God a chance to show us how strong and dependable He is in our life.

Since the Lord is always with us, leading, guarding, and loving us, let's face the challenges with bravery and thankfulness. May His delight keep us going through every hardship and remind us that we are never alone.

DEVELOPING A GENEROSITY HEART

"For where your treasure is, there your heart will be also." - Matthew 6:21 (NIV)

Knowing where our real value is is essential to cultivating a generous heart. It is vital for us to keep in mind the everlasting perspective that God asks us to embrace in a society that continuously tempts us with worldly goods and financial success.

The Matthew passage serves as a helpful reminder that the things we value most in life are what our hearts are drawn to. Greed, selfishness, and the never-ending quest for more will hold our hearts prisoner if our main goal is to amass cash and belongings for our own gain.

On the other hand, our hearts will be overflowing with love, compassion, and a desire to benefit others if our wealth is anchored in God's kingdom. A generous heart searches for chances to give our time, money, and skills to others in need, seeing beyond self-interest.

A change in priorities and a strengthening of our relationship with God are necessary for cultivating a generous heart. As we realize that investing in the eternal rather than the transient brings true joy and purpose, we start to match our goals with His.

By consciously pursuing God's will and adopting a giving lifestyle, we change our hearts to become more like Him. We take an active role in furthering His kingdom and enjoy the happiness that comes from giving without expecting anything in return. Let us try to develop a heart that generously offers people God's love and cherishes what God values.

TRUSTING GOD'S PLAN IN TIMES OF WAITING

"But they who wait for the Lord shall renew their strength; they shall mount up with wings like eagles; they shall run and not be weary; they shall walk and not faint." - Isaiah 40:31 (ESV)

Waiting might make it difficult to trust God's plan. We frequently want our prayers to be answered and resolved right away. But God's time does not always coincide with ours. The prophet Isaiah reminds us of the importance of waiting on the Lord in this passage.

Waiting on the Lord is putting our faith and confidence in Him and awaiting His direction and will with patience. Knowing that God is working behind the scenes to create His ideal plan for our life means that we should expect things actively rather than waiting passively.

We may feel worn out, exhausted, and disheartened while we wait, but God promises to give us new strength. He gives us the stamina we require to endure and keep running the course of faith. We can overcome our circumstances, diversions, and uncertainties, just like eagles fly over the sky.

God promises those who wait on Him to walk in confidence and endurance rather than to get weary. He will give us the strength to go forth with unflinching trust, sustaining us through life's obstacles and uncertainties.

Therefore, let us keep our focus on the Lord throughout these times of waiting, looking forward to His faithfulness and accepting His plan. We won't be waiting in vain because eventually He will accomplish His goals and we will regain our vigor.

ACCEPTING YOUR TALENTS' DIVINE PURPOSE

"I can do all things through Christ who strengthens me." - Philippians 4:13 (NIV)

As males, we are endowed by a loving and purposeful Creator with certain talents and abilities. However, we occasionally might wonder what good our gifts serve or whether we can carry out the intentions God has for us.

The apostle Paul teaches us a profound lesson in Philippians 4:13: with Christ's strength, we can accomplish everything. This passage is a potent reminder that God gave us our gifts for a specific reason. God provides us with the power and ability

156

needed to carry out His intentions for our life, so we are not alone in our undertakings.

Regardless of our strengths—leadership, creativity, compassion, or any other—we may approach our abilities with confidence because we know that we could change the world because of Christ. We may have faith that God will lead us, give us strength, and use our abilities to further His goals.

Rather of questioning our skills or evaluating ourselves against others, let's appreciate and acknowledge our abilities as divine gifts. As we utilize our skills to serve Him and make an effect on the world, let us look to Him for direction and rely on His power.

Gratitude fully accepts the gifts that God has given you today, knowing that you have everything you need in Christ to accomplish the divine purpose for which you were made.

DISCOVERING HEALING IN GOD'S PRESENCE

"Heal me, LORD, and I will be healed; save me and I will be saved, for you are the one I praise." - Jeremiah 17:14 (NIV)

We frequently want for healing during our brokenness, suffering, and problems. Wholeness is what we all aspire to in terms of our bodily, emotional, and spiritual well-being. But where can we get well?

We are reminded that the Lord is the source of our healing in the text above. We can cry out to Him and put our faith in His ability to deliver us from our suffering. Not only is God able, but He also wants and desires to restore our bodies, brains, and souls.

When faced with obstacles and problems, we frequently attempt to solve them on our own. We rely on our own abilities, strengths, and resources. But God asks us to come to Him because He is the only one who can truly bring us healing and restoration. Since He is the only one who can bring about healing and wholeness, He is the one we should honor.

Let us humble ourselves before the Lord in times of need, whether it is for bodily infirmities, emotional wounds, or spiritual brokenness. Let's give Him our problems and put our faith in His kindness and compassion. We can discover the real, long-lasting healing we so urgently need in His presence.

BEING CONFIDENT IN GOD

"No weapon formed against you shall prosper,
And every tongue which rises against you in
judgment you shall condemn.
This is the heritage of the servants of the Lord,
And their righteousness is from Me,"
Says the Lord." - Isaiah 54:17 (NKJV)

God promises us in this passage that He will defend us and triumph over any weapons or attacks that are directed at us. In our life as men, we could encounter difficulties, resistance, and even spiritual combat. God has assured us, nevertheless, that no weapon fashioned against us will be successful.

God says that He will put an end to any criticism or charge made against us. He has granted us the power to expose and foil the enemy's plots. As the Lord's slaves, this promise is our inheritance, grounded in the righteousness that God has bestowed upon us.

We may cling to this passage and put our faith in God's faithfulness throughout uncertain or trying circumstances. The weapons that the enemy may attempt to use against us are nothing to be afraid of since, in the end, they will fail. Rather, we may be confident that God is our guardian and advocate.

This verse should serve as a reminder to maintain our position as God's servants, confident in the knowledge that we are covered by His righteousness and that no plan devised to harm us will succeed. May us confront life's obstacles with courage, knowing that we are safe in God's unwavering love and triumph.

THE EFFECT OF GOD'S TRANSFORMING LOVE

"For I am convinced that neither death nor life, neither angels nor demons, neither the present nor the future, nor any powers, neither height nor depth, nor anything else in all creation, will be able to separate us from the love of God that is in Christ Jesus our Lord." - Romans 8:38-39 (NIV)

God's transforming love is an unbroken link that overcomes all difficulties and barriers. The apostle Paul states in this passage that he believes nothing can ever separate us from God's love, which is found in Christ Jesus.

Men sometimes experience hardships, doubts, and temptations that make us doubt God's love for us and threaten our faith. Paul's remarks, however, serve as a reminder of the timeless character of God's love. It is a love that surpasses all limitations imposed by this world, including life and death, spiritual struggles, current situations, and unpredictable futures.

God's love for us is unfailing, and that gives us peace and certainty no matter what our shortcomings, mistakes, or failures have been in the past. His love is based on His flawless character and the selfless act of sending Jesus to die in our place, not on our deeds or merit.

Let us cling to the knowledge that God's love is unwavering and steady in the midst of difficulties and uncertainties. It is a love that will always be with us and never abandon us. Therefore, let us keep in mind that nothing can keep us from the transformative love of God, which is our ultimate source of strength and hope, whether we feel overwhelmed or detached.

OVERCOMING PRIDE BY GOD'S HUMILITY

"Do not be conformed to this world, but be transformed by the renewal of your mind, that by testing you may discern what is the will of God, what is good and acceptable and perfect." - Romans 12:2 (ESV)

In a world that constantly bombards us with its values, ideologies, and temptations, it is simple to become ensnared in the trap of following its dictates. However, we are expected to a higher standard as men of God.

The verse above serves as a reminder to fight against the demands of the outside world and concentrate on renewing our thoughts in accordance with God's desire. We may confidently live according to His perfect plan and break free from conformity by seeking His truth and bringing our ideas into line with His Word.

The deliberate choice to accept God's change and reject the world's perspective is the first step toward renewal. We may determine what is right, good, and perfect in God's perspective by praying, reflecting on the Bible, and asking the Holy Spirit for help.

We need men more than ever who will not back down from a challenge and who are firmly rooted in the Bible's veracity. Let us resolve to live in accordance with His will, renew our thoughts daily, and immerse ourselves in His truth. By giving ourselves over to God's transformational power, we will be able to experience the freedom, serenity, and satisfaction that are exclusive to that state.

THE GRACE OF GOD'S DIRECTION IN MONEY

"Do not store up for yourselves treasures on earth, where moths and vermin destroy, and where thieves break in and steal." - Matthew 6:19 (NIV)

It is simple to let the chase of money consume oneself in a society where materialism and wealth gain are the driving forces. We can discover that we are always pursuing more material belongings because we think they would provide us stability and contentment. But this Matthew chapter serves as a reminder of how transient earthly goods are.

Jesus tells us not to place a high value on accumulating money and belongings. Treasures on Earth are transient and easily lost or destroyed. God's grace, on the other hand, leads us to concentrate on heavenly goods and everlasting investments.

Men are expected to manage the money that God has entrusted to us with care. This entails prudent financial management, a refusal to succumb to materialism or greed, and an understanding that God alone provides ultimate security.

God's grace helps us make prudent financial decisions by encouraging us to put charity, frugal spending, and prudent investing first. It instructs us to pursue everlasting importance and make investments in things like love, compassion, and the expansion of His kingdom.

May we always go to God for guidance while making financial decisions, accepting His wisdom and grace in resource management. Recall that genuine contentment and safety can only be attained by leading a life in harmony with God's everlasting intentions, not by amassing worldly possessions.

USING COMMUNICATION TO STRENGTHEN RELATIONSHIPS

"Let your conversation be always full of grace, seasoned with salt, so that you may know how to answer everyone." - Colossians 4:6 (NIV)

To make any connection stronger, whether it be with friends, family, coworkers, or even complete strangers, communication is essential. This passage serves as a helpful reminder of the value of words and how we utilize them while interacting with others.

Paul exhorts us to speak with love, compassion, and understanding to have discussions that are full of grace. Speaking with compassion and understanding, listening intently, and answering with decency and respect are all components of graceful communication.

Paul also exhorts us to add salt to our interactions. Salt was utilized to preserve and improve food flavor in biblical times. Similarly, the people we engage with should benefit from the vitality, encouragement, and truth that our words impart. It is our goal to talk in a way that is encouraging, therapeutic, and inspiring.

We may manage relationships with grace and sensitivity if we are deliberate in our word choice and let grace and wisdom lead our interactions. This passage serves as a helpful reminder to approach every conversation with the goal of understanding, sympathizing, and, if necessary, providing solutions. Not only do we improve our relationships with others by communicating with grace and salt, but we also become a living example of God's love and grace to others around us.

USING GOD'S GRACE TO OVERCOME REGRET

"But he said to me, 'My grace is sufficient for you,
for my power is made perfect in weakness.'
Therefore, I will boast even more gladly about my
weaknesses, so that Christ's power may rest on me."
- 2 Corinthians 12:9 (NIV)

We might feel guilty, ashamed, and disappointed
when we harbor regret, which can be a hefty load. It
may cause us to mistrust God's forgiveness and
question our own value. But the grace of God is more
than enough to outweigh our regrets.

The apostle Paul describes his personal moment of weakness and God's answer in this passage. God assured Paul that His grace was sufficient in spite of his difficulties and regrets. Paul's frailties provided the means for God's might to operate and manifest.

Our transgressions or regrets do not diminish God's grace. Rather, it is during those very moments that His strength is refined. God uses our shortcomings as a chance to show off His power and change us.

Therefore, let us celebrate our shortcomings knowing that God's grace is enough to overcome them rather than moping over our regrets. Let's give Him our regrets so that His power can operate in our lives. We can discover healing, restoration, and forgiveness because of His grace. We may go on with confidence by accepting His grace because we know that even during regret, God's might is at work in us.

LEADING A LIFE OF HOLINESS

"But just as he who called you is holy, so be holy in all you do; for it is written: 'Be holy, because I am holy.'" - 1 Peter 1:15-16 (NIV)

Every man should take seriously the call to live a holy life. As His children, God, who has called us, is holy, and He wants us to live holy lives in every way.

Being sanctified, devoted, and set apart for God's purposes is what it means to be holy. It entails leading a life that reflects His standards, character, and values and that is agreeable to Him. It entails trying to be morally upright, pure, and pure in all of our words, deeds, and ideas.

Giving up our own self-serving wants and submitting to God's will is necessary for living a holy life. It is depending on prayer, reading God's Word, and the Holy Spirit to seek His direction and empowerment daily.

Holiness is the result of God's grace at work in us, not of our own might or efforts. God shapes us into His likeness via a process of development and transformation that lasts a lifetime.

As men, let us accept the call to holiness, realizing that it is a mandate from God rather than a choice. Since everything we do is a manifestation of our love and devotion to God, let us make an effort to live holy lives.

USING GOD'S WISDOM TO NAVIGATE PARENTING CHALLENGES

"Do not be afraid or discouraged, for the Lord God, my God, is with you. He will not leave you or forsake you." - 1 Chronicles 28:20 (NIV)

Raising our children presents a myriad of difficulties and unknowns for fathers. Whether it's helping children overcome challenges in life or making tough decisions, we might frequently feel helpless and insufficient. This passage, however, urges us to put our confidence in the Lord during these trying times.

God tells us that we don't have to confront the challenges we encounter as parents in isolation. The

174

knowledge that the Lord, our God, is with us always gives us consolation. Despite our greatest difficulties, Jesus swears to never abandon us.

This passage reminds us that even in the face of the challenges of parenting, we may rely on God's knowledge, power, and direction. Knowing that God is with us and will never leave our side can provide us comfort when doubts and concerns creep in.

Therefore, let us not allow fear or discouragement to overcome us, for we have a loving Heavenly Father who is actively involved in our parenting adventure. We can face the obstacles in life with His assistance, trusting in His unwavering love and fidelity.

GIVING UP YOUR WILL IN ACCORDANCE WITH GOD'S WILL

"Therefore, I urge you, brothers and sisters, in view of God's mercy, to offer your bodies as a living sacrifice, holy and pleasing to God—this is your true and proper worship." - Romans 12:1 (NIV)

We are commanded to surrender our will and submit it to God's will on our path of faith. We are reminded of the significance of presenting ourselves to God as living sacrifices in this text from Romans. It involves giving up our goals, aspirations, and plans to fulfill His divine purpose.

Giving up our will does not imply identity loss or passivity. Instead, it is a decision to yield our life

176

to God's all-powerful direction. It is an acknowledgment that His purposes and methods are far bigger than our own. When we submit to His will, we become vulnerable to amazing gifts, development, and metamorphosis.

It is quite OK for guys to aspire and objectives in life. But it's important to keep assessing our goals in the context of God's plan. We must humbly ask for His direction in prayer and be willing to change course if He so chooses.

We enter a life of genuine worship when we surrender our will to that of God. It is an offering to honor and exalt Him of our riches, skills, and selves. Let's try to give our will up to God every day, putting our faith in His discernment and giving our wants over to His ideal plan.

RELYING ON GOD'S FAITHFULNESS DURING DIFFICULTIES

"Do not be anxious about anything, but in every situation, by prayer and petition, with thanksgiving, present your requests to God." - Philippians 4:6 (NIV)

Fear, anxiety, and uncertainty may easily take control when faced with challenges. God begs us to put our confidence in Him, even if our natural propensity is to rely on our own power and wisdom.

We are reassured in Philippians 4:6 that we do not have to bear the weight of worry. Rather, we are encouraged to use prayer and petition to bring our worries, difficulties, and obstacles before God. It is

His faithfulness and provision in the past that we are to acknowledge and acknowledge with hearts full of thankfulness when we approach Him.

To rely on God's faithfulness is to submit and be humbled. It entails acknowledging that we are powerless over life's challenges on our own and relying instead on His wisdom and strength. By doing this, we experience tranquility that is beyond comprehension.

Even in the depths of our despair, God is dependable. He is prepared to hear us out, console us, and lead us through our difficulties. As men, we must keep in mind that depending on God is a show of faith, not weakness.

So let us lay our troubles at the feet of the Lord and put our faith in His steadfast love and faithfulness. May the awareness that we serve a dependable God who will never abandon us bring us comfort.

ACCEPTING GOD'S PLAN FOR YOUR RELATIONSHIPS

"For I know the plans I have for you," declares the Lord, "plans to prosper you and not to harm you, plans to give you hope and a future." - Jeremiah 29:11 (NIV)

It is easy to become frustrated or feel hopeless when seeking deep connections. Along the road, we could encounter perplexity, rejection, or grief. God, however, serves as a reminder that He has a purpose for our life that includes building connections.

Jeremiah 29:11, the passage above, states that God has excellent intentions for us. He wants us to flourish, to be safe from danger, to have hope, and to have a future. Our interpersonal interactions are a part of this.

Occasionally, we can try to force our relationships to operate around our own needs and goals. However, if we give God our goals and believe in His perfect timing, He may bring the proper people into our lives and lead us along a road that is both fulfilling and healthy relationships.

Seeking God's wisdom, heeding His advice, and placing our trust in His flawless plan are all part of letting God lead our relationships. While things may not always be simple or easy, there may be comfort and certainty in knowing that God is in complete control of everything.

So let's accept God's design for our relationships and put our faith in His wisdom. May we seek His will and let Him lead us through the complexities of developing deep relationships with people, giving us hope for a future full of love, happiness, and satisfaction.

GOD'S HEALING TOUCH'S POWER

"For I am the LORD, your healer." - Exodus 15:26
(NIV)

It gives one peace of mind to know that our God is not only all-powerful but also a healer, especially during times of physical or mental suffering. God first appears to His people in Exodus 15:26 as Jehovah Rapha, which translates to "the LORD, your healer."

This moving verse serves as a strong reminder that God is directly involved in our recovery. He longs to make us whole again because He sees the brokenness within of us. The healing hand of God may provide consolation and hope for every kind of illness—physical, mental, or emotional.

God, in all His wisdom, understands just what we require to be healed and restored. He extends an invitation for us to bring our suffering and sorrows to Him, believing that He can heal and complete us.

Men may attempt to tough it out and deal with their problems on their own. But this passage emphasizes how crucial it is to turn to God to receive healing. With a touch that may bring deliverance and change, he is the ultimate source of power and healing.

Whatever you are going through right now, never forget that God's healing touch could bring about freedom, wholeness, and restoration. Put your faith in His tender care and let the greatest healer in the world at work in your life.

DISCOVERING JOY IN GOD'S PRESENCE

"For in him all things were created: things in heaven and on earth, visible and invisible, whether thrones or powers or rulers or authorities; all things have been created through him and for him." - Colossians 1:16 (NIV)

It is simple to lose sight of what really counts in a world full of pressures and diversions. We pursue accomplishment, attention, and material pleasures in the hopes that they will complete us and make us happy. But only in God's presence can one find genuine delight.

The passage serves as a reminder that everything was made by Him and for Him. He is the reason behind everything in this universe, both visible and invisible. This fact ought to change our priorities and point of view. Seeking our joy and purpose in God alone is the only thing we should do, rather than looking for fulfillment in transient things.

Joy in God's presence demands deliberate effort to discover. It entails making time to spend in His presence by prayer, Bible meditation, and developing a close connection. It entails giving up our wants and directing our minds to conform to His holy will.

Prioritizing God's presence in our life leads to a profound sense of happiness and fulfillment that is greater than any accomplishment in this world. God's presence gives us courage, serenity, and an everlasting perspective that helps us navigate life's ups and downs.

Thus, let us focus our hearts on God and direct our eyes towards Him. All else will fall into place as we learn to be joyful in His presence.

THE GRACE OF GOD'S BEATITUDE

"Blessed are the pure in heart, for they shall see God." - Matthew 5:8

God's promise that people with clean hearts will see Him reflects the grace of His beatitude. This stanza addresses our inner state, or the essence of who we are, in a straightforward manner. It serves as a reminder that to have a more meaningful and authentic relationship with our Creator, we must purify our hearts, which are the source of our real beliefs and desires.

Being pure in heart refers to having an authentic and true love for God that is untarnished by impurity or selfishness. It is to strive to please God above all things and to have a heart that is in line with His desire. It demands that we develop purity in our wants, motives, and ideas.

However, the benefits of having a pure heart are astounding. The curtain is lifted, and we may see God more clearly when we have a pure heart. We are given a closer look at His grandeur, a better comprehension of His nature, and a closer bond with Him.

As we endeavor to attain moral purity, let us keep in mind that we cannot attain it alone by our own efforts. We can cleanse our souls and get closer to God because of His grace. Knowing that we shall get the amazing benefit of seeing God through His beatitude, let us cling to His strength, ask for His direction, and rely on His grace.

DEVELOPING A HEART OF PERSEVERANCE

"For you have need of endurance, so that when you have done the will of God you may receive what is promised." - Hebrews 10:36 (ESV)

The furnace of endurance is where perseverance is formed. We encounter difficulties, hardships, and barriers on our spiritual path that put our perseverance to the test. However, this passage serves as a reminder that perseverance is essential, especially when faced with challenges.

Not only does endurance consist of gritting our teeth and persevering, but it also has its foundation in the understanding of God's promises. It is the unwavering conviction that God's faithfulness will keep us alive and that His promises will eventually come to pass.

Having a persevering heart is committing to carrying out God's will despite difficulties. It calls for patience with His timetable, faith in His supply, and trust in His plans.

Men are expected to take charge, meet obstacles head-on, and endure life's storms. Character is developed, faith is strengthened, and rewards are obtained with endurance.

Thus, let us set our sights on God's promises, cling to His word, and cultivate a spirit of endurance. May us never forget that when our faith is put to the test, it results in perseverance, and it is with endurance that we will be able to enjoy all the plentiful gifts that God has planned for us.

RELYING ON GOD'S SUFFICIENT PROVISION IN TOUGH TIMES

"And my God will supply every need of yours according to his riches in glory in Christ Jesus." - Philippians 4:19 (ESV)

It might be simple to give in to anxiety and hopelessness during difficult circumstances. However, we are obligated as men of faith to put our faith in our heavenly Father's provision. This passage serves as a reminder that God is both fully capable of meeting our needs and aware of them.

We can find solace in the knowledge that our God is a loving and dependable provider, even in the face of severe financial difficulties, interpersonal difficulties, or enormous impediments. Our circumstances do not restrict Him; His resources are boundless.

It's critical for males to understand that depending only on our own might can only get us so far. We are urged to rely on God's ample supply instead. This calls for submission, humility, and a strong faith in His knowledge and kindness.

Let us put our faith in Philippians 4:19 as a promise. May the knowledge that God will meet all our needs in accordance with His glory and wealth bring us serenity. We shall encounter His rich supply and learn the delight of completely depending on our dependable Provider as we rely on Him during difficult circumstances.

TRIUMPHING OVER DOUBT VIA GOD'S PROMISES

"Have I not commanded you? Be strong and courageous. Do not be frightened, and do not be dismayed, for the Lord your God is with you wherever you go." - Joshua 1:9 (ESV)

Doubt may be a powerful enemy that impedes our development and erodes our faith. It entices us to quit up, spreads misinformation, and creates doubt. God's Word, however, provides us with a potent assurance during uncertainty: to be brave and strong because He is with us.

Men may distrust their own judgment, their skills, or even God's fidelity. But because of God's constant presence in our life, rather than our own power, He urges us to be brave and strong.

We may overcome uncertainty by firmly rooted in God's promises. He gives us assurances about His loyalty, wisdom, and boundless love. Let us recall ourselves, when we are feeling doubtful, that the God who exhorted us to be courageous and unwavering is also the God who walks before us, stands by us, and goes before us.

Let us confidently announce God's promises over our life whenever uncertainty feels like it's about to overwhelm us. Knowing that we may overcome uncertainty and find victory in Him, let us lead with supernatural bravery. We can face life's uncertainties with resolute trust and confidence when we have the certainty of His presence.

LEADING WITH DIVINE COURAGE

"Be strong and courageous. Do not fear or be in dread of them, for it is the Lord your God who goes with you. He will not leave you or forsake you." - Deuteronomy 31:6 (ESV)

God asks men to be leaders of supernatural bravery in a society that frequently seeks compromise and submission. This passage from Deuteronomy serves as a reminder that God's presence and might, rather than our own, are the source of bravery.

Men have a lot on our plates when it comes to leading our families, businesses, and communities. Along the journey, anxiety, doubt, and resistance could surface. This scripture, however, reassures us that when we put our confidence in God, we need not worry.

The unshakeable belief that God is constantly at our side is the foundation of divine bravery. He walks ahead of us, guiding our steps and giving us the power, we require. His assurances that he would never abandon us provide us the courage to tackle any circumstance head-on.

Thus, let's cling to the knowledge that we are not traveling this path of leadership alone. We may lead with divine bravery when we trust on God's power and presence because we know that He will provide us the tools we need, lead us, and deliver victory in every situation.

THE EFFECT OF GOD'S MERCY

"For judgment is without mercy to one who has shown no mercy. Mercy triumphs over judgment." - James 2:13 (ESV)

The mercy of God is revolutionary. This poem serves as a powerful reminder of the transformative power of God's mercy in a culture that too frequently embraces harsh judgment and condemnation.

Men are susceptible to falling prey to critical spirits and judgmental mindsets. However, God holds us to a higher level. He shows us mercy because He is a loving and forgiving God, not because we deserve it.

Our viewpoint is altered when we see the extent of God's kindness and permit it to enter our hearts. It forces us to forgive, grace, and treat others with compassion instead of passing judgment on them.

God's mercy influences our relationship with Him as well as how we connect to others. It serves as a reminder that our connection with Him is founded on His undeserved favor rather than transactions. We experience fresh beginnings, restoration, and redemption because of His kindness.

Let us be men who, by our words, deeds, and verdicts, reflect the kindness of God. May we be compassionate, forgive, and choose love above criticism. Those around us can experience healing, hope, and transformation as we accept the impact of God's kindness.

OVERCOMING ADDICTIONS WITH GOD'S POWER

"No temptation has overtaken you except what is common to mankind. And God is faithful; he will not let you be tempted beyond what you can bear. But when you are tempted, he will also provide a way out so that you can endure it." - 1 Corinthians 10:13 (NIV)

We might feel helpless and imprisoned by addictions because they can absorb and dominate us. However, this passage serves as a reminder that, despite temptation, we have a dependable God who is at our side and offers a path out.

198

God is aware of the difficulties we encounter. He reassures us that everyone has faced temptation at some point in their lives. In our struggle, we are not alone. God's might and presence provide us the ability to triumph.

It's critical to keep in mind that God is dependable even in our darkest hours. He guarantees that we will never be tempted more than we can resist. He gives us a plan of escape, a means of escaping the temptation that stands ready to trap us.

Let us, brothers, rely on God's might to free ourselves from the bonds of addiction. We can confront our temptations head-on because of His strength because we know that He will always be there to lead and strengthen us to endure. With Him by our side, victory is within our reach.

THE BLESSING OF GOD'S HEALING MERCY

"Bless the Lord, O my soul, and forget not all his benefits, who forgives all your iniquity, who heals all your diseases." - Psalm 103:2-3 (ESV)

God's healing kindness is a priceless gift that we sometimes take for granted. He is the heavenly healer who provides wholeness and healing during our bodily and spiritual brokenness.

This passage serves as a reminder to give thanks to the Lord with all of our hearts and to never lose sight of the amazing advantages He offers. Because of His unending kindness and grace, our crimes are forgiven and our illnesses are cured.

God can cure people beyond their physical condition. He mends the harm that sin has inflicted in our spirits in addition to healing our bodies. His cure is transformational and goes beyond any worldly medicine brought about by his supernatural touch.

Let us go to the Lord with confidence and trust when we find ourselves in need of healing—whether it be spiritual, emotional, or bodily. He is the source of restoration and healing, able to restore abundant life and cure the deepest wounds.

May we be grateful for God's healing kindness and anxious to provide this wonderful gift to others in need. Let us give Him thanks for His unwavering loyalty and His abundant affection for us.

FORTIFYING FRIENDSHIPS VIA LOYALTY

"A friend loves at all times, and a brother is born for adversity." - Proverbs 17:17 (ESV)

God has given us the priceless gift of friendships, which enhances our lives. We are reminded of the value of loyalty in our relationships by this poem. True friends provide us constant love and support through good times and bad.

In a friendship, loyalty is defined as being dependable, faithful, and trustworthy. It entails going above and beyond superficial relationships and being prepared to support one another during difficult times. In the same way that a brother is destined to assist and encourage his sibling in trying times, our friendships need to demonstrate the same profound dedication to one another.

In an environment where connections can be fleeting and superficial, let us try to strengthen our friendships by fidelity. Let reliability, honesty, and trust serve as the cornerstones of our relationships. Let's be the sort of friends that don't waver and who provide support when things get tough.

Let us men seek out and nurture friendships based on trust. Let's be the sort of friends that show our brothers the love and support of Christ by showing them our undying commitment at their time of need. By doing this, we glorify God and fortify the holy ties that bind friendships.

ACCEPTING GOD'S FINANCIAL PLAN FOR YOURSELF

"Bring the whole tithe into the storehouse, that there may be food in my house. Test me in this," says the Lord Almighty, "and see if I will not throw open the floodgates of heaven and pour out so much blessing that there will not be room enough to store it." - Malachi 3:10 (NIV)

It's simple to rely on our own plans and tactics for financial success in a society where people are fixated with financial stability. This scripture, however, encourages us to accept God's financial plan for our life.

Our first fruits, or tithes, are called to be brought into God's storehouse. We show our faith in Him as the ultimate provider by doing this. It's an act of trust and obedience.

God offers unimaginable abundance when we commit to obeying His financial plan. He releases the heavens' floodgates, bestowing benefits in a multitude of ways. These benefits may not always come with money, but they still provide a sense of stability, fulfillment, and pleasure that surpasses material wealth.

Let us, brothers, put our faith in God's financial plan for us. It is He who promises to supply exceedingly and abundantly when we respect Him with our finances. May we possess the bravery to surrender our plans to Him, understanding that His supply is far more abundant than anything we could do ourselves.

HANDLING DISAGREEMENT WITH GOD'S LOVE

"A new command I give you: Love one another. As I have loved you, so you must love one another." - John 13:34 (NIV)

Conflicts will inevitably arise in life. As males, we come into circumstances in which disagreements and disputes occur. But this verse also serves as a helpful reminder of how important it is to approach conflicts with God's love.

With great wisdom, Jesus bestows upon us a new commandment: love for one another. This commandment establishes a high bar for how we need to behave toward one another, particularly when we disagree. Despite our differences, we are expected to love others as Christ has loved us.

Seeking understanding, exercising empathy, and showing grace are all part of loving one another even when we disagree. For the sake of unity, we must set aside our egos and agendas and act with patience and humility.

We cannot allow arguments to ruin our relationships as men of faith. Rather, let us approach conflicts by basing our decisions on God's love. By doing this, we may strengthen our bonds with one another, create common ground, and construct bridges.

To manage differences with grace, respect, and understanding—and ultimately, to reflect God's love to the world around us—may His love serve as a solid basis.

LETTING GO OF FUTURE CONCERNS

"Therefore, do not worry about tomorrow, for tomorrow will worry about itself. Each day has enough trouble of its own." - Matthew 6:34 (NIV)

Men are prone to carrying the load of worry about the future. Our concerns are numerous and include our jobs, money, relationships, and so on. This verse, however, serves as a helpful reminder of the significance of letting go of our hold on the unknowns of the future.

Jesus shows us that worrying about the future just makes our lives more stressful than they need to be. Rather, we are urged to live in the present and have faith that God will provide our needs every day.

Giving up on worries about the future is a sign of defeat rather than carelessness. It is a manifestation of our belief in a sovereign, benevolent God who oversees our future. Because we know that God's grace is enough for every moment, it enables us to appreciate and fully experience the present.

So let us learn to live day by day, seeking God's direction and supply for the present. We may be released from stress and live completely in the present by putting our future in His hands, knowing that our heavenly Father has already gone before us.

RELYING ON GOD'S SOVEREIGNTY DURING DIFFICULTIES

"And we know that for those who love God all things work together for good, for those who are called according to his purpose." - Romans 8:28 (ESV)

Life will inevitably involve difficulties. We experience suffering, difficulties, and tribulations that might cause us to lose faith and feel overburdened. This verse, however, serves as a reminder to put our faith in God's sovereignty and His capacity to work everything out for our benefit.

When faced with difficulties, it's natural to doubt God's purpose and ask why things are working out the way they are. However, we are expected to have confidence that God is in charge as men of faith. Every aspect of our life is being planned by Him for a reason.

We may take comfort in the knowledge that God can utilize every challenge we face to mold and perfect us, even when we are unable to see the wider picture. He can create triumph from loss, beauty from ashes, and strength from weakness.

So let us, in trying circumstances, put our trust in God's sovereignty. May we rely on Him and have faith that He is orchestrating things for our benefit, rather than allowing fear or uncertainty to overcome us. Even the most difficult situations may result in benefits and progress when they are in His hands.

DISCOVERING CALM IN GOD'S PRESENCE

"Be still and know that I am God. I will be exalted among the nations; I will be exalted in the earth!" - Psalm 46:10 (ESV)

Finding quiet times might feel like a luxury in a society when noise, distractions, and bustle are all around us. But this scripture also emphasizes how crucial it is to acknowledge God's presence and remain still.

God urges us to halt, to rest our minds, and to be still during the upheaval and confusion. Knowing that God is in charge at these times may give us a profound sense of serenity and tranquility.

We invite God's presence and let His serenity envelope us when we consciously make time to be still before Him. These are the times when we may feel His unwavering love, hear His soft voice, and find peace for our spirits.

Men are known for bearing heavy loads, obligations, and anxieties. However, we find strength and sanctuary in God's presence. He extends an invitation for us to put our confidence in His dependability and to give Him our worries.

Thus, let us consciously strive to set aside time to remain still in God's presence. May we let go of our anxieties, find comfort in His love, and experience a profound serenity that uplifts our spirits.

THE ENORMITY OF GOD'S TRANSFORMING LOVE

"But God demonstrates his own love for us in this: While we were still sinners, Christ died for us." - Romans 5:8 (NIV)

God's transformative love is so great it is incomprehensible. This one passage emphasizes God's readiness to go to tremendous measures to show us how much He loves us, which sums up God's profound love for us.

God's love is not dependent on our deservingness or morality. His love is made the more evident by the reality that we are sinners. Christ voluntarily gave His life on the cross for us when we

214

were still in a rebellious state. He showed us the height of selfless love by pursuing us even though we weren't deserving.

Realizing the extent of God's love changes us fundamentally. It mends our brokenness, pardons our transgressions, and gives our life back to us. This unmatched love gives us the ability to undergo real transformation and grow into the men God intended us to be.

Let us never undervalue the power of God's transformative love, brothers. It is a love that is unfathomable and capable of drastically altering our circumstances. May we always strive to fully comprehend the extent of His love and allow it to influence our decisions, deeds, and interpersonal interactions.

EMBRACING GOD'S PLAN FOR YOUR FAMILY

"And if it is evil in your eyes to serve the LORD, choose this day whom you will serve, whether the gods your fathers served in the region beyond the River, or the gods of the Amorites in whose land you dwell. But as for me and my house, we will serve the LORD." - Joshua 24:15 (ESV)

The task of guiding our families in the ways of the Lord has been given to us as men. We must consciously decide to accept God's plan for our families in the face of many distractions and temptations.

Joshua's verse is a potent reminder of our responsibility as spiritual leaders. Much like the people of Israel, we must decide whether to serve the Lord with all our hearts or the idols of this world.

Let us also make the same proclamation that Joshua did: "As for me and my house, we will serve the LORD." Let our houses serve as a haven where God is exalted, His Word is imparted, and His love is shown.

Let us, brothers, make it our daily goal to match God's plan for our families with our hearts and deeds. By praying, seeking His direction, and obediently following His instructions, we may leave a legacy of faith that will influence future generations. May our families serve as an example of God's grace and love, illuminating the world and bringing people to Him.

LIVING WITH GODLY CONFIDENCE

"For God has not given us a spirit of fear and timidity, but of power, love, and self-discipline." - 2 Timothy 1:7 (NLT)

Men deal with a lot of strain and uncertainty in their lives. But the Bible tells us that we are not supposed to live in timidity or fear. Because of the strength, love, and self-control that emanate from Him, we are obligated to live with a godly confidence.

God has given us His Spirit, which gives us the bravery and courage to take on any problem. This assurance comes from our Heavenly Father's power and supply, not from our own ability.

Godly faith is depending on Him in all circumstances and believing that He will fulfill His promises. It entails developing love for God and others, accepting the strength that comes from a life given over to Him, and practicing self-control to live in accordance with His will.

Let's break free from the chains of shyness and fear today. Let's use the strength, compassion, and self-control that God has bestowed upon us. We can weather the ups and downs of life with godly assurance, knowing that the One who has equipped us will never abandon us.

THE BLESSING OF GOD'S COMFORT IN LOSS

"Blessed be the God and Father of our Lord Jesus Christ, the Father of mercies and God of all comfort." - 2 Corinthians 1:3 (ESV)

Life will inevitably include loss. Grief may be quite intense, whether it is brought on by the loss of a dream, a loved one, or the end of a meaningful relationship. However, we have a God who consoles us despite the suffering.

It is said of God that He is the God of all consolation and the Father of mercies. He is aware of our deepest grief and sympathizes with us. He yearns to comfort and calm us throughout our grieving.

We can take comfort in the knowledge that God is close by, prepared to throw His loving arms around us when we are going through difficult times. His consolation is beyond our comprehension and mends our broken hearts.

Men sometimes have the tendency to mask their suffering and seem courageous. But God encourages us to bring our wounds to Him so that He might offer the consolation that only He can.

During our loss, let us take refuge in the knowledge that we serve a God who genuinely loves us, is sympathetic to our sorrow, and extends His loving presence to us.

DEVELOPING A HEART OF THANKFULNESS

"Give thanks in all circumstances; for this is the will of God in Christ Jesus for you." - 1 Thessalonians 5:18 (ESV)

It's simple to become distracted in today's environment and forget about the gifts all around us. However, this passage serves as a reminder of how crucial it is to develop an attitude of gratitude, no matter what our circumstances.

Putting forth deliberate effort is necessary to cultivate a grateful heart. It entails teaching our thoughts to remain fixed on God's kindness even in the face of adversity. It is realizing that all good originates from God and being thankful for even the little things in life.

Being thankful is a decision we make regardless of the challenges we encounter. It is not based on our situation. We may be thankful even when faced with difficulties, uncertainty, and tribulations. By being grateful, we can change our viewpoint and see that God is still at work—even in the middle of our difficulties.

Thus, let us make the decision to be grateful in any situation. May we grow to perceive God's hand at work in every area of our life and cultivate an abundantly grateful heart. Giving gratitude is a way of life that enables us to live in accordance with God's plan for our life, not merely a gesture.

RELYING ON GOD'S GUIDANCE IN MAKING DECISIONS

"Trust in the Lord with all your heart, and do not lean on your own understanding. In all your ways acknowledge him, and he will make straight your paths." - Proverbs 3:5-6 (ESV)

Men frequently have to make decisions that might have a lasting impact on their life. It is vital to rely on God's direction in these circumstances rather than our finite comprehension.

Giving up control of our own plans, preferences, and wishes in favor of the will of the Lord is a necessary part of fully trusting Him. It entails admitting that His knowledge is far greater than our own and giving Him the freedom to guide our steps.

God says He will straighten our pathways if we recognize Him in everything. Even if the road we choose may not match our own ideas or preferences, He will lead and guide us.

So let's ask God for wisdom before making any decisions. Let us rely on His knowledge and put our faith in His wisdom. May we give up the desire to dictate our own fates and submit to His ideal plan for our life. By doing this, we will be acting in accordance with God's will, which will bring us clarity, calm, and confidence.

EMPOWERED BY GRACE: DISCOVERING THE STRENGTH IN GOD'S FREE FAVOR

"But he said to me, 'My grace is sufficient for you, for my power is made perfect in weakness.' Therefore I will boast all the more gladly of my weaknesses, so that the power of Christ may rest upon me." - 2 Corinthians 12:9 (ESV)

We might easily lose sight of the tremendous power found in God's grace in a society that frequently prizes independence and self-reliance. This passage serves as a reminder that we are empowered in our moments of weakness by God's favor, which is freely provided via His grace.

God's grace is independent of our deservingness or achievements. It is an unmerited gift that is not deserving. And this grace has a spiritual force that helps us overcome the obstacles in life.

Rather from being a cause for shame, our shortcomings serve as platforms for God's might to be seen. His power may be seen in us when we accept our limits and rely on His grace.

Brothers, let us accept the power that comes from God's unmerited goodness. During our times of weakness, let us exalt God's favor rather than trying to improve ourselves. We can confidently confront any challenge when we rely on His power because we know that it will carry and sustain us.

GOD'S AFFIRMATION: OVERCOMING INSECURITY

"So we can confidently say, 'The Lord is my helper; I will not fear; what can man do to me?'" - Hebrews 13:6 (ESV)

Many guys struggle with insecurity; they continuously feel unqualified and uneasy in several facets of life. However, this verse is a potent reminder that we can overcome uncertainty when our confidence is based in God.

It gives us comfort and confidence to know that the Lord is our advocate. We have nothing to be afraid of since He is on our side. When we acknowledge the existence and assistance of our

228

Heavenly Father, the views and verdicts of others have no influence on us.

Seeking approval and validation from people on earth is a common cause of insecurity, but genuine affirmation can only come from God. Upon placing all our faith in Him and His steadfast love for us, we can overcome timidity.

Brothers, let us focus more on God's truth than on human opinion. His praises are more powerful than any voice that attempts to undermine us. When the Lord is on our side, we may stand tall in the knowledge that we are safe in His love, approved by Him, and prepared to face any insecurities down the road.

UNLIMITED LOVE: WITNESSING GOD'S POWER THROUGH HIS INDESTRUCTIBLE LOVE

"And I am convinced that nothing can ever separate us from God's love. Neither death nor life, neither angels nor demons, neither our fears for today nor our worries about tomorrow—not even the powers of hell can separate us from God's love." - Romans 8:38 (NLT)

The love of God is boundless, unfathomable, and unbreakable. It is an unending love that endures in all circumstances. This passage serves as a reminder that nothing in all of creation can ever keep us from the unconditional love of our Heavenly Father.

We frequently want for a love that is unwavering and unfailing in a world full of brokenness, suffering, and uncertainty. It is filled with God's love. When everything else fails, love endures unwaveringly.

God's love endures no matter what we go through, even the deepest depths, the hardest fights, and even our own uncertainties and fears. Love is stronger than all other emotions, even the darkest ones.

As males, it is both our honor and duty to demonstrate God's mighty might via His unbreakable love. The knowledge that God's love is boundless and unfailing should give us courage. In the name of the One who first loved us, may us spread this love to everyone in our vicinity, bringing hope, healing, and restoration.

GOD'S WISDOM'S BLESSING IN RELATIONSHIPS

"Above all else, guard your heart, for everything you do flows from it." - Proverbs 4:23 (NIV)

It's important to follow God's guidance and keep our hearts safe in all our relationships, romantic and platonic. This verse serves as a reminder that our words, ideas, and deeds all flow from our hearts. As such, shielding our hearts from harmful influences and toxic routines is crucial.

God's wisdom offers discretion and insight to manage relationships in a positive and satisfying way. It instructs us to emphasize love and forgiveness, to speak honestly and openly, and to value and respect others.

Being mindful of the influences we let into our life, such as the people we choose to surround ourselves with, the media we consume, and the places we choose to hang out with, is essential to protecting our hearts. It entails establishing limits and being conscious of how our deeds and attitudes affect the health of our partnerships.

Brothers, while we negotiate the intricacies of relationships, let us seek God's guidance. May we protect our hearts, submitting them to His direction so that His grace and love might pass through us. We may enjoy the benefits of happy, healthy relationships when we connect our hearts with God's.

GOD'S DESIGN: STRENGTHENING MARRIAGES

"Husbands, love your wives, just as Christ loved the church and gave himself up for her." - Ephesians 5:25 (NIV)

God created marriage as a holy relationship, and as husbands, it is our responsibility to uphold this commitment. This verse serves as a reminder to love our spouses in the unselfish, self-sacrificing manner that Christ demonstrated for the church.

In our marriages, males are expected to follow Christ's example. Christ's love voluntarily gave up all for the sake of the church's expansion and well-being; it was not conditional or dependent on convenience.

Similarly, we ought to love our spouses without conditions and prioritize their needs over our own. In the same way that Christ served, we are to treasure and guard them.

We strengthen and resiliently support marriage when we accept God's purpose for it. By putting our spouses first and showing selfless love, we foster an atmosphere of closeness, security, and trust.

As Christ loves the church, let us always aim to love our spouses. May our marriages provide as a solid basis for development, harmony, and joy—a mirror of God's love and kindness.

CONQUERING FEAR WITH GOD'S UNWAVERING LOVE

"There is no fear in love. But perfect love drives out fear because fear has to do with punishment. The one who fears is not made perfect in love." - 1 John 4:18 (NIV)

Fear is a strong feeling that can prevent us from moving forward and immobilize us. It speaks falsehoods, assures us that we are incapable, and sows doubt in our souls. However, this passage serves as a reminder that fear cannot overcome God's unfailing love.

There is no place for fear to reside in God's pure love. Fear begins to fade from our hearts as we realize how much He loves us. We come to understand that we have a loving Father who is watching over and protecting us—we are not alone.

As men, we can confront our concerns with courage because we know that we can conquer any challenges because of God's love. Our identity is derived from the love and strength of our God, not from our worries.

Let's resist giving in to the fearful voices that want to stop us. Rather, let us accept the flawless love of our Heavenly Father and allow it to dispel our fear and give us the confidence and fortitude to move forth. God's unfailing love empowers us to overcome every obstacle in our path.

LEADING A PURPOSEFUL LIFE

"And he has given him authority to execute judgment, because he is the Son of Man." - John 5:27 (ESV)

Men frequently find themselves looking for direction and meaning in life. Our goal is to have an impactful and meaningful life that makes a difference. Jesus tells us in this passage that since He is the Son of Man, He has the right to administer judgment.

The first step in realizing our mission is acknowledging that we are God's children, called by God to serve. As offspring of the Highest, we too are granted authority, just as Jesus was.

We must connect our emotions and actions with God's will if we are to live a worthwhile existence. It is our honor to positively impact people' lives and to embody God's justice and love in all we do.

We have the power to lead, effect permanent change, and create good change because of Jesus. As men of God, let us accept our role and use our skills and talents to honor God and contribute to the establishment of His Kingdom on Earth.

USING GOD'S WISDOM TO NAVIGATE PARENTING DIFFICULTIES

"If any of you lacks wisdom, let him ask God, who gives generously to all without reproach, and it will be given him." - James 1:5 (ESV)

As dads, we might occasionally feel unqualified and uncertain about the best choices to make for our kids. But as this passage makes clear, God is a freely giving source of insight. We can pray to Him and ask for His direction when we don't understand.

The wisdom of God surpasses our finite comprehension. It provides us with perceptions, judgments, and answers that are beyond our comprehension. He pledges to give insight to anybody who asks, without holding back or passing judgment.

Let us acknowledge the necessity of God's guidance in our parenting path. Rather than depending exclusively on our own comprehension, let us humble ourselves and pursue His direction. He will give us the discernment required to handle the trials and tribulations of parenting as we communicate with Him.

We can confidently lead our families, make informed decisions, and create loving, godly homes when we use God's knowledge as our compass.

GIVING UP WANTS TO FOLLOW GOD'S WILL

"Then Jesus told his disciples, 'If anyone would come after me, let him deny himself and take up his cross and follow me.'" - Matthew 16:24 (ESV)

Men are known for having strong passions and aspirations. Our goals are enjoyment, comfort, and success. But this verse also serves as a reminder that doing God's will means letting up of our own wishes.

True discipleship requires us to deny ourselves. This entails setting aside our personal goals, worldly desires, and plans. It entails realizing that God's ways are superior to ours and that, in the end, His plan for our life is superior to anything we could ever want.

Accepting our cross represents our readiness to make sacrifices to advance the gospel. It may include letting go of material belongings, pride, or comfort. Living in accordance with God's purpose necessitates a complete surrender of our will.

Brothers, let us embrace the invitation to fully follow Jesus rather than letting our own desires rule our lives. To live a life acceptable to God, may we deny ourselves, take up our cross, and give up our desires. We shall reap the bountiful benefits of walking in His will when we do this.

RELYING ON GOD'S UNWAVERING FAITHFULNESS DURING ADVERSITY

"The steadfast love of the Lord never ceases; his mercies never come to an end; they are new every morning; great is your faithfulness." - Lamentations 3:22-23 (ESV)

There are many highs and lows, wins and losses, pleasures and tragedies in life. It's simple to feel overwhelmed and lose hope when faced with hardship. However, this passage serves as a reminder of God's constant faithfulness, even under the most difficult circumstances.

Whatever we go through, God's love never wavers. His mercies never expire and are renewed every morning. He is incredibly dependable; it never wavers or fails. We may depend on God's unwavering love and fidelity even in the face of uncertainty in the world.

It is essential to keep in mind that God is at our side throughout difficult times. He never falters in His presence or in His promises. Knowing that He will never leave us gives us courage and peace.

Let us, brothers, place our faith in God's unwavering constancy. Let us cling to His promises and find solace in His love during difficult times. Every storm will pass, and His faithfulness will lead us to triumph.

ACCEPTING GOD'S DESIGN FOR YOUR SOCIAL CIRCLES

"So then, as we have opportunity, let us do good to everyone, and especially to those who are of the household of faith." - Galatians 6:10 (ESV)

Men tend to be picky about the individuals they spend their time with. People with comparable interests, ideals, or histories may tend to attract us. This verse, however, serves as a reminder of how crucial it is to accept God's plan for our social networks.

God commands us to treat everyone we encounter compassion and kindness. While it's simple to love those who are like us, we also have a duty to extend love and support to those who may be different. Our brothers and sisters in Christ are included in this.

It is essential to cultivate wholesome connections inside the home of religion. In our spiritual path, we are to uplift, assist, and encourage one another. These connections provide us a concrete expression and aid in our spiritual development of God's love.

Let's not confine the people in our social circles to only those who share our interests. Rather, let us deliberately strive to go outside our comfort zones and show love to everyone. We may experience the richness and diversity of the body of Christ via sincere relationships and by continuing to be receptive to God's direction.

THE HEALING POWER OF GOD'S TOUCH

"No temptation has overtaken you that is not common to man. God is faithful, and he will not let you be tempted beyond your ability, but with the temptation he will also provide the way of escape, that you may be able to endure it." - 1 Corinthians 10:13 (ESV)

Addictions have the power to take hold of our life and imprison us in a destructive cycle of conduct. However, this passage gives us hope and serves as a reminder that we are not facing our problems alone. God reassures us that everyone has encountered temptation; we are not alone in our struggles.

Our mooring during addiction is God's steadfast love. He guarantees that he won't subject us to temptation that we can't withstand. He offers a means of escaping the clutches of addiction, which is our source of strength.

We may experience times of weakness and temptation in our quest to beat addiction. But we may take solace in the knowledge that God is by our side the entire time, providing His strength and grace to assist us withstand the lure of our vices.

We can escape the bonds of addiction with the help of God. As we travel the road of healing, let us rely on His dependability, hold fast to His promises, and ask for His direction. We are able to achieve restoration, healing, and a life free from the shackles of addiction because of His strength.

DISCOVERING HAPPINESS IN GOD'S PRESENCE

"Happy are the people whose God is the Lord!" - Psalm 144:15 (NKJV)

We frequently seek to outside sources of satisfaction, like relationships, achievement, or material belongings. But happiness that lasts, genuine happiness, can only be experienced in the presence of God.

According to this scripture, people who have their hearts fully committed to the Lord are genuinely fortunate and content. Making God the focus of our life, seeking His will and walking in His ways, results in a profound and satisfying satisfaction that outweighs any fleeting enjoyment this world can provide.

Accepting our relationship with God is the first step toward finding contentment in His presence. By developing a strong and intimate relationship with our Creator, we open ourselves up to a source of happiness that transcends transient situations.

Whatever difficulties or tribulations we may encounter, God's presence offers consolation, serenity, and unfailing delight. As we discover the real enjoyment that can only be experienced in His presence, may we continuously seek His face and match our hearts with His.

THE GRACE OF GOD'S FORBEARANCE

"But God demonstrates his own love for us in this:
While we were still sinners, Christ died for us." -
Romans 5:8 (NIV)

The idea of God's grace and patience is astounding and inspirational. This line from Romans serves as a reminder of God's unfathomable love for us, which is shown in the atonement of His Son, Jesus Christ.

God's love is not dependent upon our perfection or righteousness. Indeed, God extended His grace to us precisely because of our sinful situation. Christ voluntarily gave His life in order to save us when we were still deeply in sin.

This poem is a potent reminder of God's love's breadth and depth. It demonstrates His kindness and endurance toward us despite our shortcomings and errors. It is evidence of His steadfast commitment and His yearning for peace.

May we never underestimate God's generosity of patience. Let us seek to live in a way that reflects the sacrifice made on our behalf while humbly accepting His pardon. We are given the hope, healing, and transformation that only He can give by His grace.

FOSTERING A PERSISTENT HEART

"For God gave us a spirit not of fear but of power and love and self-control." - 2 Timothy 1:7 (ESV)

We are commanded, as men of faith, to have an unshakeable, persistent heart that seeks God's will for our life. This verse serves as a reminder that God has endowed us with the spirit of strength, love, and self-control, giving us the ability to persevere through trials and maintain our faith.

In an uncertain world, dread may seize hold of our emotions with ease. However, we are reminded that a believer's life is devoid of dread. We may face our worries and venture fearlessly into the unknown because God's strength resides inside us.

God's loving experiences give us the courage and tenacity to keep going. Even when everything seems against us, we can persevere because of His unwavering love. This love is what keeps us going and gives us the willpower to keep moving forward.

In addition, God has given us the ability to exercise self-control. With the help of this gift, we can control our thoughts, feelings, and behavior and make moral decisions that please God. We acquire endurance and resilience in the face of adversity by self-control.

Let us cultivate a heart that is unwavering, grounded in the might, love, and restraint of God. As we negotiate life's challenges, may we overcome our anxieties, accept His love, and practice self-control.

RELYING ON GOD'S SUSTENANCE DURING DIFFICULT TIMES

"And my God will supply every need of yours according to his riches in glory in Christ Jesus." - Philippians 4:19 (ESV)

Sometimes unanticipated obstacles and problems in life leave us feeling helpless and unclear of how to move forward. It is important to keep in mind that we are not alone at such moments. God promises to provide all our wants out of His boundless love and generosity.

This Philippians passage gives us comfort in knowing that our heavenly father is aware of our wants and provides for them with enough. God's boundless resources are made accessible to us via Christ Jesus, whether it be in the form of counsel, financial help, physical strength, or emotional support.

God's constancy and the breadth of His love for us are brought to light when we rely on Him for our nourishment in trying times. It shows us that even in seemingly hopeless situations, we may put our faith in His time and provision.

Males may experience a range of hardships that put our faith to the test. Let us, however, put our faith in God's sustaining power and allow Him to be our strength and refuge in the middle of everything. Knowing that He will always provide for us allows us to truly discover strength and serenity.

CONQUER DOUBT BY FAITH IN GOD'S PROMISES

"Now faith is the assurance of things hoped for, the conviction of things not seen." - Hebrews 11:1 (ESV)

Being a persistent foe, doubt may infiltrate our thoughts and sow doubtful thoughts. It has the power to shatter our faith and steal the joy and serenity that come from putting our confidence in God's promises. However, this verse serves as a reminder that uncertainty may be vanquished by faith.

Faith is confidence and conviction in things hoped for but not yet seen; it is not blind. It is a strong conviction that God keeps His word, especially in the face of seemingly unfavorable circumstances.

We must consult God's Word and remind ourselves of His unwavering faithfulness whenever doubts creep in. We may turn to Him for direction, cast our uncertainties before Him, and put our faith in His promises when we're feeling unsure.

We may overcome doubt by faith and enjoy the serenity, happiness, and assurance that come from trusting in God's Word. Let us never stop strengthening our faith, which is based on the promises made by our obedient God, and walking in the certainty of His unwavering love.

EXHIBITING GODLY COURAGE

"Be strong and courageous. Do not be afraid; do not be discouraged, for the Lord your God will be with you wherever you go." - Joshua 1:9 (NIV)

Men frequently encounter difficulties and unknowns that might make us feel anxious and disheartened. However, this passage from Joshua reminds us that when God is in our life, we may have access to a fearless spirit.

God Himself commands us to be strong and bold; it is not only a recommendation. He exhorts us to have courage and to keep going on despite our fears and discouragements. Why? Because no matter where our path takes us, He remains by our side the entire time.

We put our confidence in the certainty that we serve a strong, faithful, sovereign God when we act with godly bravery. By having faith in His unwavering presence, we may summon the courage to confront our anxieties, get over roadblocks, and welcome the opportunities that life presents.

Let's push over our fears and uncertainty and confidently pursue the goals God intends for our life. We can face our anxieties, traverse the unknown, and carry out our purpose with unshakeable bravery and confidence when the Lord is by our side.

THE SIGNIFICANCE OF GOD'S MERCY

"For I desire steadfast love and not sacrifice, the knowledge of God rather than burnt offerings." - Hosea 6:6 (ESV)

It is simple to place exterior acts and religious rituals above the state of our emotions during life's chaos. However, this passage from Hosea clarifies what God values most of all.

God wants real love, not just token offerings. He yearns for a sincere bond based on mercy, love, and compassion with every one of us. He prefers a heart that goes beyond merely doing religious rituals to know Him deeply.

The importance of God's kindness is immeasurable. It serves as a reminder that God's mercy is always available to us, regardless of how far we may have gone or how many mistakes we have committed. It is a gift that ushers in fresh starts, forgiveness, and repair.

As men, let us seek a genuine and profound connection with God rather than only concentrating on outward displays of piety. May we be merciful to others, loving and caring for others in whatever we do. May we be shaped by the importance of God's kindness and undergo an inward transformation.

OVERCOMING ADDICTIONS BY FAITH IN GOD'S POWER

"For everyone born of God overcomes the world.
This is the victory that has overcome the world,
even our faith." - 1 John 5:4 (NIV)

Addictions have the capacity to be strong, consuming, and crippling. They have the power to imprison and powerless us. However, God tells us in this passage that we can conquer any challenge in this life, even addiction, if we have faith.

Our success depends on our confidence in God's ability. We have the fortitude and resiliency to face the temptations and difficulties the world presents to us because we are born of God. This triumph is the result of our constant faith in God, not our own might or determination.

Let's rely on God's strength and grace in the face of addiction. We may break free from the bonds of addiction and achieve freedom and healing if we base our actions on our beliefs. Although the journey may present challenges, we may have confidence that our trust in God's ability will enable us to overcome our obstacles. Let's cling to this pledge while we bravely pursue our recovery from addiction.

THE BENEFIT OF GOD'S HEALING PRESENCE

"He heals the brokenhearted and binds up their wounds." - Psalm 147:3 (ESV)

God's presence is a genuine, palpable reality that promotes healing and rebuilding, not merely a consoling idea. We are reminded of the immeasurable advantages of God's healing presence in this line from Psalm 147.

Our hearts are frequently scarred by the sorrows, anguish, and disappointments of the past because we live in a broken and wounded world. However, God does not abandon us in our sin. He is the ultimate healer, prepared to bandage our wounds and cure our broken hearts.

God heals the deepest parts of our souls with His love, kindness, and mercy. He is sympathetic to us and is aware of our suffering. We discover a shelter in His presence, where His divine touch heals our wounds and transforms our brokenness into wholeness.

God's healing presence brings hope and restoration to those who struggle with emotional scars, relationship brokenness, or spiritual emptiness. Seeking His presence will enable Him to mend and revitalize every aspect of our existence. As God mends our wounded hearts, may we know the transforming power of His love.

USING LOYALTY TO STRENGTHEN FRIENDSHIPS

"A friend loves at all times, and a brother is born for adversity." - Proverbs 17:17 (ESV)

God has given us the priceless gift of friendship. They have the power to uplift, comfort, and support us. This Proverbs passage serves as a helpful reminder of the value of loyalty in establishing and preserving these kinds of connections.

Genuine friendship transcends fleeting relationships. A faithful friend is someone we can always count on to be there for us in good times and bad. They are there to share in our successes and provide support when we need it most.

We are expected to be devoted friends as guys. Our devotion may act as a stabilizing force for people around us in a society where connections are often erratic and short-lived. Our steadfast dedication and support are what allow us to create enduring connections.

Let's foster relationship loyalty by being dependable, unselfish, and trustworthy. May we go above and above to be the kind of friends that God has shown us, showing them our love and concern. Loyalty can help us forge enduring ties with our friends that will honor God and make our lives more fulfilling.

ACCEPTING GOD'S PLAN FOR YOUR FINANCIAL SITUATION

"And my God will supply every need of yours according to his riches in glory in Christ Jesus." - Philippians 4:19 (ESV)

Anxiety and tension are frequently brought on by our financial status. Our concerns can include reaching our financial objectives, supporting our family, or just barely scraping by. This text from Philippians reminds us that God has promised to supply all our needs in the midst of these worries.

God, who is rich and glorious in plenty, is not unaffected by our financial hardships. He promises to use His boundless resources to provide for all of our needs. We may rely on Him to provide all our needs—daily needs, unforeseen costs, and our deepest aspirations.

Giving God control over our fears and anxieties is necessary to accept His plan for our financial circumstances. It entails admitting that God is in charge and that He has prepared a special gift for every one of us.

And let us take solace in the knowledge that God is our ultimate provider, even while we seek His wisdom and direction in handling our finances. He leads the way, clearing the path for abundance, provision, and financial security. We might find serenity, happiness, and a greater dependence on His dependable care when we put our trust in His resources.

HANDLING DISAGREEMENT WITH GOD'S LOVE

"A new command I give you: Love one another. As I have loved you, so you must love one another." - John 13:34 (NIV)

Conflicts and disagreements will always arise in our relationships—with God and with other people. But we are called, as men of faith, to treat these differences with the love that God has demonstrated.

Jesus offers us a new commandment in this verse: to love one another. He establishes the norm for how we ought to handle conflicts: with love, just as He has loved us. This love is unselfish, compassionate, and forgiving; it does not require agreement or consensus.

We can react with pride, wrath, or rage when confronted with opposing ideas. But in keeping with Jesus' example, we must answer in a loving manner. We may reduce tensions, promote understanding, and work toward unanimity in the face of conflict by doing this.

Recall that our capacity to show love to those with whom we disagree is an indication of our own love for God. Love, grace, and respect for others are how we obey His mandate and let His love show through in our lives. May we approach conflicts with the kindness and humility that come from knowing and becoming followers of Jesus.

LETTING GO OF FUTURE CONCERNS

"Do not be anxious about anything, but in everything by prayer and supplication with thanksgiving let your requests be made known to God." - Philippians 4:6 (ESV)

Men are frequently overcome with anxieties and anxieties about what lies ahead. We could be concerned about our relationships, income, careers, or health. But God is calling us to put our faith in Him and let go of our fears.

This text from Philippians urges us to offer our worries to God via prayer rather than letting them worry us. We are exhorted to make requests of Him, to communicate our wants and requirements while keeping an attitude of gratitude.

We acknowledge God's sovereignty and our capacity to be guided and provided for when we give Him our anxieties. The knowledge that nothing is too large or little for Him to manage gives us comfort. He is always ready to hear our petitions and to answer them.

It takes faith to let go of worries about the future and to trust in God's knowledge and purposes. Knowing that He is in control allows us to feel at ease and confident when we give Him our anxieties. Have trust in His fidelity and find solace in the knowing that He is watching out for us.

RELYING ON GOD'S AUTHORITY IN DIFFICULTIES

"But he said to me, 'My grace is sufficient for you,
for my power is made perfect in weakness.'
Therefore, I will boast even more gladly about my
weaknesses, so that Christ's power may rest on me."
- 2 Corinthians 12:9

We frequently feel helpless and overwhelmed when faced with obstacles and problems. However, this passage urges us to submit to God's rule and remain still. He is the all-powerful God who rules everything, and He maintains control even when we face difficulties.

It is simple to depend on our own fortitude and wisdom when faced with challenges and uncertainty. But this passage asks us to stop, to still our emotions, and to confess that God is in charge. We can feel secure and at ease in His rule.

Let's remind ourselves of God's strength and constancy when things get tough. In addition to working for our benefit and His glory, He is elevated above all peoples and the surface of the whole planet. To get past our difficulties, we may put our trust in His authority.

May we give God our problems, recognizing His power and putting our faith in His perfect plan. Knowing that He is with us every step of the journey gives us the strength to conquer challenges as we relax in His presence.

DISCOVERING CALM IN GOD'S PRESENCE

"Be still and know that I am God. I will be exalted among the nations; I will be exalted in the earth!" - Psalm 46:10 (ESV)

It might be difficult to find a sense of tranquility in our hectic, fast-paced environment. We are overloaded with obligations, demands, and diversions that tug on us in all directions. But in the middle of this chaos, God extends an invitation for us to find serenity in His presence.

We are reminded to stay calm and acknowledge that God exists in this line from Psalm 46. We can genuinely feel God's serenity and repose in the

278

silence, in the peaceful moments of stop and contemplation. A deliberate period of stillness before Him might help us to escape the cacophony of the world around us.

We may feel secure knowing that our All-Powerful God is in charge while we are in His presence. He is elevated above all, and we find peace and comfort in His might and majesty. Let us make quiet and silence a priority so that God can speak to our hearts and envelop us in His serenity. We can experience a peace that is beyond comprehension while we are in His presence.

THE TRANSFORMATIVE POWER OF GOD'S LOVE

"For I am sure that neither death nor life, nor angels nor rulers, nor things present nor things to come, nor powers, nor height nor depth, nor anything else in all creation, will be able to separate us from the love of God in Christ Jesus our Lord." - Romans 8:38-39 (ESV)

There are no boundaries to God's love's transformational power. This passage from Romans serves as a reminder that nothing in this world can ever separate us from God's boundless, consuming love.

It gives us comfort to know that God's love is unchanging and unyielding, even in times of uncertainty, fear, or despair. It embraces us with His grace and salvation from the bottom of our hearts.

God's love has the power to change our lives, mend our brokenness, and rekindle our hope. It transcends all conditions on earth and overcomes all barriers.

As males, we may experience hardships, setbacks, or times of vulnerability. However, let us cling to the knowledge that God's love transcends all that we experience. His love has the capacity to bring about rejuvenation, change, and a happy, fulfilling existence.

Accept the transforming force of God's love and let it influence all facets of your life. Allow His love to direct your choices, mend your scars, and give you the strength to live a life that exemplifies His kindness and generosity.

GOD'S FORGIVENESS AS A MEANS OF OVERCOMING BITTERNESS

"Be kind to one another, tenderhearted, forgiving one another, as God in Christ forgave you." - Ephesians 4:32 (ESV)

When we refuse to forgive and hang onto grudges, bitterness may seep into our hearts. It eats away at us gradually, corrupting our relationships and impeding our personal development. However, God provides us with forgiveness as a cure for our resentment.

This text exhorts us to emulate God's forgiveness, which He showed by offering His Son, Jesus Christ, as a sacrifice. We are commanded to treat people with kindness, tenderness, and forgiveness, just as God has done for us.

We may release ourselves from the weight of resentment by making the decision to forgive. It is a way for us to go past the cycle of resentment and heal. However, it's not always simple to forgive. It takes courage, humility, and the knowledge that God has pardoned us all as well.

Let us look to God's example of forgiveness when our own bitterness threatens to overwhelm us. By His grace, may we show forgiveness to those who have harmed us, and in doing so, may we conquer resentment and discover the life-changing potential of God's forgiveness.

LIVING WITH GODLY CONFIDENCE

"For God has not given us a spirit of fear, but of power and of love and of a sound mind." - 2 Timothy 1:7 (NKJV)

Being a man of faith requires having a Godly confidence in one's life. This passage from 2 Timothy serves as a reminder that God has given us a spirit of strength, love, and good reasoning rather than one of dread.

Men frequently have difficulties, doubts, and even insecurities that can erode their self-assurance. But God's might remind us that our identity is founded in God's power, not in fear. We can confront any circumstance with bravery and boldness because He is inside us.

We can overcome our inadequacies and uncertainties because of God's love. We may walk with renewed confidence when we accept His love because we know that our Heavenly Father values and cherishes us.

God also gives us a clear intellect, enabling us to make decisions with clarity, knowledge, and insight. We may put our confidence in His direction, knowing that He will guide us in the correct direction.

Let us live confidently in God, depending on His strength, love, and wisdom. May us walk with confidence and bravery, understanding that we are strengthened by the All-Powerful God who is constantly by our side.

THE GIFT OF GOD'S SOLACE IN GRIEF

"Even though I walk through the valley of the shadow of death, I will fear no evil, for you are with me; your rod and your staff, they comfort me." - Psalm 23:4 (ESV)

A journey through dark and bitter valleys is what grief is. Our hearts bleed currently, and our souls yearn for solace. God promises to be there and to provide comfort during such grief.

The psalmist reminds us that God is with us, so we need not fear, even in the darkest depths of despair. He is our everlasting friend, using His staff and rod to lead and shield us. Even in the worst hours, his very presence is consoling and peaceful.

We may take comfort in knowing we are not alone when sadness feels like it could consume us. God is there to walk with us down the valley, providing His love and support at every turn.

Whether it's the loss of a dream, the breakup of a relationship, or the death of a loved one, males can experience sadness. Let us hold on to the assurance of God's presence throughout these trying times and take solace in His unfailing love. He is our stronghold and haven, our constant support throughout difficult times.

DEVELOPING AN APPRECIATIVE HEART

"In every situation, no matter what the circumstances, be thankful and continually give thanks to God; for this is the will of God for you in Christ Jesus." - 1 Thessalonians 5:18 (AMP)

Aligning ourselves with God's plan for our life is a transforming discipline of cultivating a grateful heart. Regardless of the challenges we may encounter, this passage exhorts us to practice thankfulness in all circumstances.

This passage serves as a helpful reminder to change our perspective because it is sometimes simpler to concentrate on the things we lack or the difficulties we face. We are commanded to praise God for what we do have rather than focusing on what we lack.

Having an appreciating heart is a decision we make every day, regardless of the situation. It recognizes God's goodness and faithfulness in the face of adversity. It fosters a sense of happiness and helps us see the gifts we might have missed.

Let us men make a commitment to cultivating an attitude of gratitude. May we always be grateful to God and delight in His grace and provision. Gratitude may cause a deep inner transformation that opens our hearts to receive God's kindness in all areas of our life.

RELYING ON GOD'S INSIGHT WHEN MAKING DECISIONS

"For the Lord gives wisdom; from his mouth come knowledge and understanding." - Proverbs 2:6 (NIV)

Making decisions may be difficult, particularly when they are significant decisions that affect our lives. It is vital for us as men to rely on God's wisdom in these circumstances.

We are reminded that real wisdom originates from the Lord in this Proverbs passage. He is the wellspring of wisdom and insight. We may make confident judgments when we seek His guidance and conform our hearts to His desire.

God's wisdom is beyond our finite comprehension. He understands what is best for us and has a broad perspective. We can make sense of the complicated things in life and go forward with clarity when we rely on His knowledge.

Let us men humble ourselves and confess that we need God's wisdom. Rather of depending exclusively on our own comprehension, let us pursue His knowledge by prayer, reading His Word, and consulting with experienced Christians.

We may put our faith in God to direct our actions and set us on the correct course when we make decisions based on His wisdom. May we always rely on His discernment and follow His direction in every area of our life.

ACCEPTING GOD'S WILL FOR YOUR FAMILY

"Commit your way to the Lord; trust in him, and he will act." - Psalm 37:5 (ESV)

Determining God's plan for our families can be challenging when faced with the intricacies and obstacles of family life. This line, however, serves as a reminder of how crucial it is to entrust our family's journey to the Lord.

The ultimate planner and mentor for our families is God. He understands what is best for us and has a broad perspective. We show our faith in His knowledge and omnipotence when we give Him control over the goals, aspirations, and objectives of our family.

While putting our trust in God does not ensure that we will never face difficulties or challenges, it does assure us that He will intervene on our side. He will reveal His perfect will for our families via working in surprising ways.

We can find comfort in the knowledge that God is in charge and has a plan for our family. We make room for His direction, guiding, and benefits when we give Him our plans. May we put our faith in God's plan for our family and find comfort in His tender supervision.

THE EFFECT OF THE ALMIGHTY LOVE OF GOD

"For I am convinced that neither death nor life, neither angels nor demons, neither the present nor the future, nor any powers, neither height nor depth, nor anything else in all creation, will be able to separate us from the love of God that is in Christ Jesus our Lord." - Romans 8:38-39 (NIV)

God's love is an infinite energy that goes into the deepest recesses of our being, overcomes all barriers, and transcends all powers. We are reminded of the amazing impact that God's love has on our lives by this verse from Romans.

There is nothing that can ever separate us from God's consuming love. Not even spiritual powers bent on destroying us or death. Nothing can sever God's love for us, no matter how difficult or unpredictable the situation may be.

Our lives are significantly impacted when we fully comprehend the breadth and depth of God's love. It provides us strength when we're weak, consolation when things are hard, and a feeling of direction and hope.

God's omnipotent love is transforming; it has the capacity to alter us within. Men, let us embrace this unwavering love and let it mold who we are, direct our actions, and motivate us to love others with the same radical, unconditional abandon.

OVERCOMING UNCERTAINTY WITH GOD'S VALIDATION

"He will make straight your paths." - Proverbs 3:6 (ESV)

Frequently, uncertainty may make us feel disoriented and uneasy about the future. However, this passage serves as a reminder that we are not alone in navigating life's unpredictable roads. God promises to straighten our pathways when we ask for His direction and put our confidence in Him.

We may have to make decisions that seem overwhelming or ambiguous on our spiritual path. We could experience uncertainty and anxiety. But certainty and serenity come from God's approval and guidance.

God lines our paths with His perfect will when we give Him our goals and aspirations. He gives us guidance, clarity, and reassurance that we are headed in the correct route.

Let us prioritize seeking God's affirmation above anything else during uncertain times. We can trust that He will guide us along the route that leads to satisfaction and purpose when we use Him as our compass. Put your faith in His knowledge, rely on His insight, and let Him direct your actions. God's approval causes doubt to vanish, and navigating life takes on a divinely purposeful adventure.

THE ADVANTAGE OF GOD'S INSIGHT IN PARTNERSHIPS

"Do not be unequally yoked with unbelievers. For what partnership has righteousness with lawlessness? Or what fellowship has light with darkness?" - 2 Corinthians 6:14 (ESV)

In our journey through life, we often form partnerships and connections with others. In all areas of life—business, friendships, and relationships—we must seek God's guidance and surround ourselves with like-minded people.

This passage emphasizes how crucial it is that we choose our companions carefully. Being "unequally yoked" refers to forming a relationship with someone who does not hold the same values as us. Such alliances have the potential to turn us from holiness and jeopardize our relationship with God.

God's wisdom gives us a leg up in collaborations. Aligning oneself with like-minded individuals allows us to support one another's spiritual development, hold one another responsible, and work toward shared objectives that exalt God.

To ensure that we surround ourselves with people who will encourage, inspire, and push us to live out our faith, let's seek God's wisdom and discernment in our partnerships. We may enjoy the fullness of God's blessings and do great things for His kingdom when we band together with like-minded others.

SPIRITUAL WARFARE AND STRENGTH

"For the weapons of our warfare are not of the flesh but have divine power to destroy strongholds." - 2 Corinthians 10:4 (ESV)

Men are called to use the powerful weapons that God has supplied in the fight against the spiritual powers of darkness. Our spiritual determination might be weakened by temptations, pressures, and challenges in this world of ours. But do not be alarmed; we possess supernatural might to vanquish any fortress.

As men, we must understand that our strength is not derived from our own skills or experience. Instead, it results from a steadfast trust in God and a dependence on His Spirit. This passage serves as a reminder that our weapons are supernatural rather than material. God's Word, prayer, and the armor He supplies are what give us power.

We need to put on all of God's armor, cling firmly to His truth, and wield the sword of the Spirit if we want to win spiritual battle. We are called to walk in the freedom and power that Jesus Christ has given us, to oppose the enemy's plans, and to destroy strongholds.

I hope this scripture will always serve as a reminder that we are not fighting this battle alone. When heavenly force is on our side, we may triumph in the spiritual war we fight daily by being resilient and overcoming all challenges.

OVERCOMING FEAR WITH GOD'S PERFECT LOVE

"Perfect love drives out fear." - 1 John 4:18a (NIV)

Fear may easily seize hold of our hearts and prevent us from pursuing our God-given mission in a world full of doubts and fears. But the complete love of our Heavenly Father gives us comfort and courage as men of faith.

The passage from 1 John serves as a reminder that God's love knows no bounds or restrictions. His love is all-encompassing, flawless, and unwavering. Fear no longer has the same influence over our life when we genuinely realize how much He loves us.

We have the option to cling to God's love rather than give in to fear. Prayer, introspection on His Word, and developing a close connection with Him help us to overcome fear and enter the brave, courageous, and confident realm that results from realizing our perfect God's love for us.

Let us not let fear stand in the way of our advancement or divert us from God's purpose for our life. Seize hold of His flawless love and see how fear begins to fade, enabling us to live successful lives based on steadfast faith in the One who loves us infinitely.

LEADING A PURPOSEFUL LIFE

"Blessed is the man who trusts in the Lord, whose confidence is in Him." - Jeremiah 17:7 (NIV)

It is simple to forget our actual mission as men in a world full of diversions and conflicting goals. God wants our lives to matter, rooted in Him and directed by His purposes for us.

The Jeremiah passage reminds us of the blessings that result from putting our faith and trust in the Lord. He reveals His plan for our life when we submit to His will, providing us with fulfillment and direction that beyond our comprehension.

Cultivating a strong and steadfast confidence in God is the first step towards living a purposeful life. Because of this faith, we can ask for His direction in all spheres of our lives, including relationships, work, and personal development.

Men are expected to intentionally connect their decisions and behaviors with God's calling on their lives. Through prayer and Bible study, we may understand His plans and make decisions that are honoring to Him.

When we give our lives to the Lord, we can enjoy His direction, favor, and contentment while living meaningful lives that have an influence on everyone around us.

THE BLESSING OF SATISFACTION IN GOD'S WILL

"Blessed is the man who walks not in the counsel of the wicked, nor stands in the way of sinners, nor sits in the seat of scoffers; but his delight is in the law of the LORD, and on his law he meditates day and night." - Psalm 1:1-2 (ESV)

It seems hard to attain true joy in a world full with diversions and temptations. But as men of faith, we have the amazing chance to live in accordance with God's plan and enjoy the great benefit of fulfillment.

The psalmist says that people are very blessed if they take pleasure in God's law and think about it

306

every day. Seeking the will of our Heavenly Father will satisfy us more than pursuing worldly interests or abiding by the wicked ways of the world.

Our hearts are changed as we spend time in God's Word and conform our beliefs and behavior to what He says. We start to experience a level of fulfillment and contentment that much outweighs the transient joys that come from earthly endeavors.

Our lives become clearer and more purposeful when we live according to God's will. It provides access to happiness, tranquility, and a closer bond with our Creator. Let us humbly seek God's will as we confront life's obstacles, allowing His direction to bring us into the contentment and fullness that are exclusive to Him.

PUTTING YOUR TRUST IN GOD'S CAREER PLAN

"Commit your way to the Lord, trust also in Him, and He shall bring it to pass." - Psalm 37:5 (NKJV)

It is easy for men to get obsessed with the pursuit of their own job goals in a world where success and ambition are the defining characteristics. But we are called to approach our professional life differently as Christ-followers. It is our duty to rely on God's professional plan.

We are reminded to commit to the Lord and put our confidence in Him in Psalm 37:5. God is the one who ultimately leads our steps and sets the road for us, even though we may have our own goals and wishes. He completes our plans in ways that beyond our wildest dreams when we give Him our goals.

Letting go of our own will and seeking God's direction via prayer and Bible study are necessary for trusting in God's professional plan. It entails putting His will ahead of our own and having faith that He is aware of what is best for us.

Let's give God our fears and anxiety over our future careers today. Let's give up on our goals, ask for His direction, and have faith that He will guide us along a route that precisely fits His plan for our life.

MANAGING CHANGE WITH FAITH IN GOD

"Trust in the LORD with all your heart and lean not on your own understanding; in all your ways submit to him, and he will make your paths straight." - Proverbs 3:5-6 (NIV)

Because things change so quickly and conditions might change without warning, it is normal for males to feel uneasy and overwhelmed. But as men of religion, we have an obligation to face change with steadfast confidence in God.

The Proverbs passage serves as a helpful reminder to rely on the Lord rather than our own wisdom. Our trust in God's knowledge and direction ought to be our steadfast foundation during times of uncertainty and change. He urges us to believe in His flawless plan and surrender our ways to Him.

Knowing that God is with us every step of the way allows us to welcome the chances that come with change rather than fighting it or giving in to fear. By praying, seeking His direction, and coordinating our deeds with His Word, we may confidently manage life's complexity.

Men, let us never forget that change presents a chance for development and rejuvenation. We may discover courage, discernment, and serenity in the face of change if we firmly rely on our faith and give God control over our plans.

GIVING UP WORRIES TO GOD'S CALM

"Cast all your anxiety on him because he cares for you." - 1 Peter 5:7 (NIV)

It is all too easy for fear and anxiety to take over our hearts and brains in a world that is chaotic and uncertain. The burden of obligations, doubts, and problems might make us feel overburdened. But as men of religion, we have God as a strong source of support and tranquility.

We are reminded of God's immense love and concern for each one of us in 1 Peter 5:7. We are urged to give our cares and concerns to Him, putting them in His capable hands, and to throw our troubles upon Him. When we give God our problems, we take solace in His serenity and encounter an unfathomable peace.

Rather of assuming the weight of concern on our own, we are encouraged to have faith in God's fidelity and provision. Letting go and putting all of our confidence in Him is a purposeful choice. We learn that God is in charge and that His perfect peace is watching over our hearts and thoughts when we let go of our anxieties.

Knowing that God is sincerely concerned about us, let's choose today to surrender our anxieties to His serenity. May the knowledge that God is constantly with us provide consolation and cast a shadow over any anxiety that seeks to take control of our life.

THE STRENGTH OF GOD'S TRANSFORMATIVE GRACE

"But he said to me, 'My grace is sufficient for you,
for my power is made perfect in weakness.'
Therefore, I will boast even more gladly about my
weaknesses, so that Christ's power may rest on me."
- 2 Corinthians 12:9 (NIV)

We frequently try to rely on our own power and talents when we are weak. But the Bible tells us that God's grace is enough for us. We have the honor to encounter God's grace's transformational power during our vulnerable times.

Men can experience the burden of meeting social norms and the need to be resilient in all facets of their lives. However, the kindness of God calls us to swallow our egos and acknowledge that we are not superhuman. Our frailties make His strength flawless.

This passage exhorts us to accept our flaws rather than run away from or reject them. Recognizing our limits allows us to be more receptive to God's grace and power. We are regenerated, transformed, and given the ability to accomplish His goals by His grace.

Instead of taking pride in our own abilities, let's celebrate the power of God's transforming grace at work inside us. May the knowledge that His grace is adequate for every difficulty we encounter bring us peace and hope.

RESOLVING REMORSE VIA GOD'S ATONEMENT

"If we confess our sins, He is faithful and just to forgive us our sins and to cleanse us from all unrighteousness." - 1 John 1:9 (NKJV)

A man's heart might be greatly burdened by regret and remorse, which can fill him with guilt and humiliation. However, we are not supposed to bear the burden of our previous transgressions by ourselves as Christ-followers. God's kindness and forgiveness provide us with a road out of regret and toward healing.

We are reminded of the value of confession and the certainty of God's pardon in 1 John 1:9. God is loyal and just to pardon us when we really acknowledge our fault and humble ourselves before Him. He compassionately purges us of all wickedness rather than holding our sins against us.

The only way we may finally be freed from the regret that consumes our souls is by God's atonement. We may give up our regrets and allow His grace to change our hearts and thoughts as we accept His pardon.

Let us confess our sins, regrets, and remorse to the Lord today. May we be grateful for God's pardon and experience the freedom and serenity that come from His atonement rather than dwelling on our past transgressions.

DISCOVERING HAPPINESS IN GOD'S EVERYDAY BLESSINGS

"Rejoice always, pray without ceasing, in everything give thanks; for this is the will of God in Christ Jesus for you." - 1 Thessalonians 5:16-18 (NKJV)

It's simple to forget the daily benefits that God gives us during life's chaos. This devotional encourages men to develop an attitude of thankfulness and discover enduring joy in the little things that God provides for us.

Regardless of the situation, the scripture from 1 Thessalonians exhorts us to constantly be joyful. We may change our perspective from what we need to what God has kindly supplied by choosing joy. We are reminded to keep in touch with our Heavenly Father during the day by praying to Him and communicating with Him often.

Furthermore, the passage emphasizes that offering thanks is God's wish for us, teaching us the important lesson of gratitude. We may develop a heart of satisfaction and discover enjoyment in even the tiniest moments when we recognize and give thanks for the little things in life that surround us.

This devotional encourages men to take a moment to consider how God benefits them daily, which helps them develop a grateful attitude and find genuine enjoyment in these small acts of kindness.

THE BENEFIT OF GOD'S DEPENDABILITY IN CONNECTIONS

"Two are better than one, because they have a good reward for their labor." - Ecclesiastes 4:9 (NKJV)

One thing is certain in a society where connections can be erratic and relationships frequently fail: God is trustworthy and faithful in every one of our interactions. This Ecclesiastes verse serves as a helpful reminder of the importance and advantages of traveling through life with a trustworthy partner.

Men tend to strive to handle tasks and obligations by themselves, yet God intended for us to be social beings who connect with one another.

Having dependable people by our side gives us the bravery, support, and strength we need to tackle any challenge.

God's reliability in our interactions with one another extends beyond interpersonal ties. He pledges to accompany us on every step of the journey, offering knowledge, consolation, and direction. All other relationships are supported and enhanced by our relationship with Him.

God has arranged relationships for us; let's treasure and invest in them, delighting in the benefits they offer. As we go through life together, we may enjoy the benefits of camaraderie, support from one another, and progress because of our dependence on Him and the gift of trustworthy connections.

FOSTERING A GENEROUS HEART

Each of you should give what you have decided in your heart to give, not reluctantly or under compulsion, for God loves a cheerful giver." - 2 Corinthians 9:7 (NIV)

Men need to develop a giving heart that is like our Heavenly Father's in a society where people are obsessed with obtaining, owning, and heaping. This text from 2 Corinthians serves as a helpful reminder that donating is a chance to show God's love in our life rather than merely fulfilling a task or responsibility.

Giving voluntarily and joyfully is God's will, not forcing us to contribute unwillingly or under duress.

Giving from a generous heart unites us with God's heart and makes us conduits for His gifts to others.

Developing a giving heart requires a change of viewpoint. It entails realizing that everything we own, including our time, skills, and finances, is really a gift from God. We may approach giving with thankfulness, enthusiasm, and a desire to positively influence other people's lives when we view it through this lens.

As men, let's try to provide an example of generosity by giving of ourselves to our families, communities, and the less fortunate in addition to our material possessions. May we plant seeds of charity, kindness, and compassion, showing God's love in all we do.

RELYING ON DIVINE GUIDANCE FOR PARENTING

"Train up a child in the way he should go, and when he is old, he will not depart from it." - Proverbs 22:6 (NKJV)

It is our duty as men to lead and serve as examples for our families, particularly when it comes to parenting. However, parenting children may be an intimidating undertaking, leaving us unsure of how to mentor and instruct them.

The necessity of teaching our children the way of the Lord is emphasized throughout God's Word. Godly principles and genuine training may have a lasting effect on their lives, as Proverbs 22:6 reminds us.

We must keep in mind that we are not alone in our efforts to be good parents. We have access to divine counsel that is prepared to enable and empower us to carry out this great duty. We may successfully traverse the pleasures and trials of parenting children if we seek knowledge from God, rely on His support, and make decisions that are consistent with His Word.

This verse should act as a continual reminder to us to dedicate ourselves to teaching our children godly values, knowing that our efforts will benefit them and leave an enduring legacy.

ACCEPTING YOUR TALENTS' DIVINE PURPOSE

"Each of you should use whatever gift you have received to serve others, as faithful stewards of God's grace in its various forms." - 1 Peter 4:10 (NIV)

God has given every one of us special gifts and capacities. But occasionally, we might find it difficult to acknowledge or embrace their divine purpose for us. We can be skeptical of their worth or our capacity to change things.

However, we are obligated to use our abilities for the good of others as men of faith. We are reminded to faithfully manage the grace that we have received from God in 1 Peter 4:10. It exhorts us to use our gifts for the good of others around us and the honor of our Creator.

By accepting the heavenly intent behind our gifts, we may help establish God's kingdom on earth. Our gifts—whether they be in compassion, creativity, teaching, or leadership—have been given to us for a purpose.

Let's stop doubting and undervaluing the gifts that God has given us. Rather, let us accept them with humility and thankfulness, anxious to utilize them to change the world for the better and leave a lasting impression on others.

GOD'S TRANSFORMING LOVE'S IMPACT

"And we all, with unveiled face, beholding the glory of the Lord, are being transformed into the same image from one degree of glory to another. For this comes from the Lord who is the Spirit." - 2 Corinthians 3:18 (ESV)

Our lives can be drastically changed by the love of God. Our hearts and minds are saturated with His presence when we genuinely experience His glory, and we start to emulate Him.

This transition is a continuous process rather than a one-time occurrence. We gradually undergo internal transformation as we persistently seek God's face and reflect on His Word. Each day that goes by, we are being shaped more and more into the image of Christ.

God's transformative love is clearly at work in our relationships, decisions, and dispositions. It modifies our viewpoint, giving us a heavenly prism through which to see the world. It gives us the ability to provide people unconditional love, forgive others as we have been forgiven, and show kindness and grace to everyone in our path.

Let's accept the ability of God's love to transform today. May we experience His ongoing activity in our lives as we keep our eyes fixed on Him, becoming more and more like Him, and spreading His love to a world in need.

GOD'S HUMILITY'S POWER TO OVERCOME PRIDE

"God opposes the proud but gives grace to the humble." - James 4:6 (NIV)

Our relationships with God and other people may be hampered by pride, a misleading and harmful force that is easy to let into our hearts. It prevents us from seeing our own shortcomings, isolates us from the knowledge of others, and impedes our development of humility.

But in His infinite wisdom, God provides us with humility, a potent remedy for arrogance. God opposes the arrogant but gives ample grace to the humble, as James 4:6 tells us.

We ought to imitate our Heavenly Father's humility as men walking in faith. We become vulnerable to God's grace's transformational power when we accept humility. Being humble enables us to serve with honesty and compassion, to value others above ourselves, and to acknowledge our need for God.

Refrain from allowing pride to mislead you. Rather, accept the humility that Christ embodied, for it is via humility that we encounter God's power in its entirety in our lives. Let us humble ourselves before God and give up our arrogance, relying on His grace to lead and mold us into men of real character.

GOD'S BLESSINGS IN FINANCIAL GUIDANCE

"Honor the Lord with your possessions, and with the firstfruits of all your increase; so your barns will be filled with plenty, and your vats will overflow with new wine." – Proverbs 3:9-10 (NKJV)

Men must go to God for direction and give Him our best resources to achieve wealth and financial security. The world frequently tempts us to place our faith in worldly goods, riches, and prestige. But genuine financial rewards come from setting our thoughts and deeds in line with God's will.

The Proverbs passage emphasizes the promises from God that come with being a good steward. God promises to richly bless us when we make it a priority to glorify Him with our belongings, whether that means paying our tithe, donating liberally, or handling our money sensibly.

God wants to bless us abundantly in every aspect of our life, including money. He will lavish His benefits upon us as we obediently follow His commands, putting our faith in His supply and utilizing our resources for His purposes.

Let us seek solace in this potent scriptural truth, depending on God's direction and supply. We should view financial stewardship as a chance to glorify God, understanding that riches and benefits flow from a heart that is devoted to giving Him our all.

GOD'S GRACE TO OVERCOME REGRET

"For I will forgive their wickedness and will remember their sins no more." - Hebrews 8:12 (NIV)

We might carry a great deal of regret in our hearts and brains. We could find ourselves stuck in a vicious cycle of shame and remorse, wishing we could go back in time and fix the errors or chances we've lost. But there is a way out of this trap provided by God's love.

The Hebrews passage serves as a reminder of God's boundless forgiveness and kindness. He is willing to forgive our transgressions and set us free

334

from the clutches of remorse when we approach to Him in honest repentance.

Rather of wallowing in our previous transgressions, we are to accept God's forgiveness and His pledge to forget our sins. He gives us a second chance, and with His assistance, we may get over our regrets and live hopeful, meaningful lives.

Let us humbly accept God's pardon and let His grace turn our regrets into chances for development and atonement. We can discover healing, restoration, and the will to live a life free from the shackles of regret thanks to His power.

TO LIVE A LIFE OF HOLINESS

"But just as he who called you is holy, so be holy in all you do; for it is written: 'Be holy, because I am holy.'" - 1 Peter 1:15-16 (NIV)

We are called to strive holiness as men who want to live lives that please God. Everyone who is a Christian and has been called by God is entitled to holiness. Perfectly holy as He is, our Heavenly Father longs for us to emulate Him in every area of our life.

Peter tells us in this passage that God's holiness is the source of our own called to holiness. We honor and love God when we conduct our thoughts, attitudes, and deeds in accordance with His truth and righteousness.

It takes intentionality and a humble dependence on the direction and strength of the Holy Spirit to live a holy life. It entails trying to stand out, avoiding worldly temptations, and actively seeking holiness.

Let us dedicate ourselves to the quest of holiness, understanding that it is a lifelong process. To respect and exalt our holy God, may this scripture serve as a daily reminder for us to work toward holiness in our thoughts, words, and deeds.

COURAGEOUS HONESTY: FOCUSING THE STRENGTH FROM MAINTAINING A LIFE OF TRANSPARENCY AND CHARACTER

"The integrity of the upright guides them, but the unfaithful are destroyed by their duplicity." - Proverbs 11:3 (NIV)

It takes tremendous bravery to live an open and truthful life in a world full of lies and ulterior motives. Men are expected to be honest individuals who steadfastly uphold the truth and morality.

According to Proverbs 11:3, maintaining our integrity keeps us on the straight and narrow and directs us toward righteousness. When we make the decision to be honest in all aspect of our life, we are fortified by the force of genuineness, laying the groundwork for mutual respect and trust.

It might be difficult to live a transparent life. There might be pressure on us to compromise our morals or cover up our flaws. However, when we decide to live a life of uncompromising integrity and sincerity, we shine a light on a world that yearns for genuineness.

This verse should inspire us to pursue integrity fearlessly since it is both necessary for our own spiritual health and God's pleasure. Let's put our trust in His power to get through the difficulties and try to live honorably in all facets of our lives.

GOD'S WISDOM TO NAVIGATE PARENTING CHALLENGES

"For the Lord gives wisdom; from His mouth come knowledge and understanding." - Proverbs 2:6 (NIV)

There are several obstacles that men encounter in their jobs as dads. At times, being a parent can feel overwhelming as we try to make the greatest choices for our kids' development and well-being. We must keep in mind that we have access to a source of wisdom that is greater than our own comprehension during uncertain times.

According to Proverbs 2:6, the Lord is the source of real wisdom. We access an unending supply of wisdom and insight when we ask for His direction. Let us look to God's Word for guidance and understanding as we negotiate the challenges of parenting.

We can find solutions to the problems we confront by studying, praying, and relying on God's knowledge. Let's put our faith in God's direction to provide us with the means to accomplish our goals, whether they are imparting moral principles, communication skills, or discipline.

Let's reflect on this scripture and ask the Holy Spirit to accompany us on our parenting journey today. May us seek God's wisdom, trusting that He can help us overcome any obstacle in our path.

GIVING UP WANTS TO ACCEPT GOD'S WILL

"Trust in the Lord with all your heart and lean not on your own understanding; in all your ways submit to him, and he will make your paths straight." - Proverbs 3:5-6 (NIV)

Men tend to have their own goals, ambitions, and desires. But to grow spiritually and connect with God's purpose for our life, we must let go of our desires and accept His plan.

We are reminded to put all our reliance in the Lord in Proverbs 3:5–6. It calls us to surrender to His knowledge and direction rather than relying on our own understanding. We make room for Him to guide and bless us when we voluntarily give up our desires to Him.

Accepting God's will call for an active commitment to seeking His direction in all facets of our life, not a passive or complacent attitude. We feel genuine fulfillment when our aspirations are in line with His intentions and plans, and we are shown His faithfulness in guiding us along straight pathways.

As men, let us decide to submit to God's will and let up of our own desires. We may confidently face life's obstacles by fully believing Him and yielding to His guidance, knowing that His perfect plan is being revealed to us.

RELYING ON GOD'S FIDELITY DURING DIFFICULTIES

When you pass through the waters, I will be with you; and when you pass through the rivers, they will not sweep over you. When you walk through the fire, you will not be burned; the flames will not set you ablaze." - Isaiah 43:2 (NIV)

We frequently encounter difficult situations in life that put our faith and fortitude to the test. Overwhelming difficulties might make us feel forlorn and powerless. But even in the face of adversity, we who are men in Christ have the unshakeable confidence that God's faithfulness will not waver.

God has promised to be with us through the deepest waters and the fiercest fires, as Isaiah 43:2 reminds us. He will safeguard and lead us now, just as He did for His people in the past. Even if the difficulties may seem overwhelming, we may have faith that we will overcome them and come out stronger.

Let us keep this passage in mind when we face difficult circumstances. It inspires us to put our faith in God's constant love and presence. We may trust that He will uphold us and give us the bravery and fortitude to persevere even in the face of overwhelming situations.

I hope this passage always reminds us that we are not struggling alone. Our mooring, which keeps us firm among life's storms, is God's faithfulness.

ACCEPTING GOD'S DESIGN FOR YOUR RELATIONSHIPS

Husbands, love your wives, just as Christ also loved the church and gave Himself for her." - Ephesians 5:25 (NKJV)

Relationships are carefully crafted by God to represent His grace and love. Men are obligated to follow His plan for interpersonal relationships, especially when it comes to marriage.

It is important to remember that men are expected to love their wives in a selfless manner, just as Jesus loved the church, according to Ephesians 5:25. This text exhorts us to serve and dedicate ourselves to our wives, following Christ's example of sacrificial love.

To embrace God's plan for our marriages, we must respect and treasure our women as priceless gifts from above. We can foster an environment of togetherness, trust, and support by doing deeds of love, kindness, and surrender.

Let us always seek God's wisdom and direction in fostering our marriages, as we endeavor to live every day as examples of Christ's love. Our relationships will blossom and exalt God's name as we relinquish our own preferences and wishes and allow His love to flow through us.

This scripture should inspire us to accept the divine plan that God has for our marriages and to rely only on His power to carry out our responsibilities as spouses and husbands.

THE STRENGTH OF GOD'S RESTORATIVE HANDS

"He heals the brokenhearted and binds up their wounds." - Psalm 147:3 (NKJV)

We are prone to being broken down by life, leaving us injured and in pain. We want for healing and restoration while bearing the wounds of previous transgressions, setbacks, and suffering. However, optimism remains.

Psalm 147:3 gives us comfort and confidence in God's ability to heal. He is the heavenly Healer who binds our wounded souls and tenderly heals our shattered hearts. God's touch offers consolation, strength, and rejuvenation when we feel broken and shattered.

We are prone to being broken down by life, leaving us injured and in pain. We want for healing and restoration while bearing the wounds of previous transgressions, setbacks, and suffering. However, optimism remains.

Psalm 147:3 gives us comfort and confidence in God's ability to heal. He is the heavenly Healer who binds our wounded souls and tenderly heals our shattered hearts. God's touch offers consolation, strength, and rejuvenation when we feel broken and shattered.

DISCOVERING HAPPINESS IN GOD'S PRESENCE

"You make known to me the path of life; in your presence there is fullness of joy; at your right hand are pleasures forevermore." - Psalm 16:11 (ESV)

We frequently look for fulfillment in a variety of endeavors, including relationships, achievement, monetary goods, and worldly pleasures, in our quest for happiness. However, happiness that is genuine and long-lasting can only be found in God's presence.

Psalm 16:11 tells us that we find the way of life and the fullness of delight when we are in God's presence. While the world may provide momentary joys, true contentment that transcends situations and fleeting wants can only be found in communication with our Creator.

God fills us with His delight and gives us the pleasures that last forever when we turn our hearts to Him and seek His presence. Our happiness stems from our relationship with Him, and nothing compares to the closeness and joy that come from being in His presence.

Men, let us make seeking God, being in His presence, and developing our relationship with Him our top priorities. Through this journey, we will uncover the real meaning of happiness, strengthening our faith and fundamentally altering our way of life.

THE GRACE OF GOD'S FORBEARANCE

"The Lord is not slow to fulfill his promise as some count slowness, but is patient toward you, not wishing that any should perish, but that all should reach repentance." - 2 Peter 3:9 (ESV)

God's boundless love for us is profoundly demonstrated by His grace of patience. He waits patiently, knowing that everyone would eventually come to know Him and experience His redemption, despite our shortcomings and mistakes.

In a society that frequently expects instant satisfaction and speedy outcomes, we might easily lose hope as we wait for our prayers to be answered or for things to become better. However, this passage serves as a reminder that God works on a schedule that is beyond our comprehension.

His seeming delay is a sign of His kindness and love. He wants everyone to have the chance to come to Him in repentance, receive forgiveness, and find reconciliation with Him.

As men, let us welcome God's favor of patience into our own lives and show it to others. May we have patience as we travel this path of faith, relying on His dependability and understanding that His timing is ideal. And while we wait, let's spread His love and the good news of salvation to help others discover the rich life that Christ has to offer.

A WARRIOR'S REST: IDENTIFYING RESISTANCE IN GIVE UP AND DEPENDING ON GOD'S LEADING

"Trust in the Lord with all your heart and lean not on your own understanding; in all your ways submit to him, and he will make your paths straight." - Proverbs 3:5-6 (NIV)

Men are frequently motivated by a deep desire to succeed and dominate. To overcome obstacles, we try to rely on our own fortitude, discernment, and comprehension. Occasionally, though, this independence might stand in the way of feeling God's heavenly guidance in our life.

Proverbs 3:5–6 serves as a reminder to let go of our tight hold on authority and put all of our confidence in the Lord. We make room for the straight, intentional, and triumphant road He has planned for us when we give up our own understanding and submit to His will.

As men of faith, we could face obstacles along the way that entice us to quit up. But we may recognize when our dependence on our own knowledge is getting in the way of following God's instructions by using discernment and carefully evaluating our hearts.

This verse should be a potent reminder to us to give up control, rely entirely on God, and find comfort in His guiding presence.

DEVELOPING A HEART OF PERSEVERANCE

"Let us not become weary in doing good, for at the proper time we will reap a harvest if we do not give up." - Galatians 6:9 (NIV)

As men of faith, we frequently encounter hardships, obstacles, and disappointments that could try our perseverance. It is at these times that we must develop a heart of endurance.

Galatians 6:9 exhorts us to keep up our good deeds and not give up. It serves as a reminder that we should never give up on our pursuit of justice, fairness, and compassion—no matter what obstacles we encounter. We are urged to persevere and not give up, even in situations when we might not see results right away or feel that our efforts are paying off.

Reliance on God's grace, fortitude, and resolve are necessary for perseverance. It means persevering through adversity, clinging to God's promises, and having faith that He will eventually bring about a harvest.

This scripture should give us hope today because it assures us that the work we accomplish for the Lord is not in vain. May we embrace a heart of endurance and tap into the power of the Holy Spirit to experience the many benefits that God has in store for us.

RELYING ON GOD'S PROVIDENCE IN TOUGH TIMES

"And we know that all things work together for good to those who love God, to those who are the called according to His purpose." - Romans 8:28 (NKJV)

We frequently face tough and demanding moments in life. We might have difficulties, failures, or unforeseen events that depress or overwhelm us. It is vital that, in these times, we as men recognize and rely on God's providence.

As Christians, we are reassured by Romans 8:28 that everything works for our benefit. God is still at work during hardships, directing events for our ultimate good and His purpose. God's providential design for our life can only be unlocked by our loyalty and love for Him.

Even while we might not always understand why bad things happen, we can find comfort in the fact that God is in charge. He is dependable to see us through every trial and provide us with guidance. Knowing that everything will work out in accordance with His perfect will allows us to find calm and hope when we put our confidence in His sovereignty.

This verse should inspire us to rely on God's providence throughout difficult times, believing that even during adversity and uncertainty, He is acting in our best interests and achieving His divine objectives.

LIVING WITH DIVINE COURAGE

"Be strong and of good courage, do not fear nor be afraid of them; for the Lord your God, He is the One who goes with you. He will not leave you nor forsake you." - Deuteronomy 31:6 (NKJV)

Men encounter difficulties and problems all the time, which can make us feel scared and uneasy. Life's stresses might occasionally lead us to doubt our own skills and self-worth. But the Bible exhorts us to live with supernatural bravery.

We are told that the Lord, our God, is with us in Deuteronomy 31:6. He is our dependable friend, our pillar of support, and our haven during difficult times.

Thus, nothing that comes our way should intimidate or cause us dread.

Courage starts to build up within of us as we depend on His promises and put our confidence in His presence. Because we know that God is constantly with us, leading, protecting, and strengthening us, we may confront the unknown with bravery.

Let this text be a continual reminder that we have access to supernatural bravery whenever we need it to navigate life. Set aside your worries for God, the Lord, will never abandon you. Move on fearlessly and greet every day with the strength of divine bravery.

THE SIGNIFICANCE OF GOD'S MERCY

"But God, who is rich in mercy, because of His great love with which He loved us..." - Ephesians 2:4 (NKJV)

There is no calculating the importance of God's kindness. He offers us His tender kindness in spite of our brokenness and unworthiness. With boundless compassion, our God extends to us his pardon, grace, and restoration.

God's mercy is derived from His boundless love for us, as Ephesians 2:4 tells us. It is something He freely gives to us rather than something we may earn or deserve. We are humbled and overcome with appreciation when we realize the extent of this kindness.

It is imperative that we men realize the full extent of God's kindness in our lives. It forces us to live obediently so that His kindness might change us from the inside out. In our relationships, we are to reflect God's mercy, giving others around us second opportunities, forgiveness, and compassion.

God's kindness should never be taken for granted; rather, we should accept it with wonder and respect. May it encourage us to walk in humility, kindness, and grace, showing others the limitless compassion of our Heavenly Father and modeling the mercy we have received.

OVERCOMING ADDICTIONS WITH THE MIGHT OF GOD

"I can do all things through Christ who strengthens me." - Philippians 4:13 (NKJV)

Addictions may have a strong hold on us, negatively impacting our mental, emotional, and spiritual health. They may make us feel helpless and confined. But we are not left to fight these battles by ourselves as men of faith.

Philippians 4:13 serves as a reminder of the extraordinary power that results from our connection with Christ. We can conquer the obstacles of addiction that appear insurmountable because of His strength. God's might is made perfect in our weakness, so we don't need to rely on our own human resources or willpower.

We must give our problems to God in order to escape the grip of addiction, asking for His direction, forgiveness, and healing at every turn. He can give us the willpower to resist temptation, adopt better lifestyles, and achieve real freedom.

Keep in mind that we have authority over addiction. We have the power of Christ's love and might, and we are sons of the Almighty, filled with the Holy Spirit. Put your faith and strength in Him, and observe as the bonds are shattered and victory is achieved.

LAST WORDS

As this amazing 180-day adventure draws to a close, we have seen God's transforming power at work in and through our lives. We have been favored with a fleeting but profound inspiration moment every day that has lifted our spirits and strengthened our souls.

We have discovered throughout these devotions that genuine power originates from a sincere desire to know God and submitting our life to His plan. We have come across ageless truths, promises, and lessons from His Word in as little as three minutes a day, and they have the power to mold our purpose, relationships, and character.

It is simple to become overwhelmed by life's responsibilities and hectic schedule in this fast-paced world, leaving little time for spiritual upkeep. For this reason, the purpose of these devotions is to give a little yet powerful dosage of God's guidance and inspiration.

As we come to an end to our voyage, let us remember these teachings. Let's sow the inspiration seeds we've been given and watch them blossom and produce fruit in our lives. Let us be men who make an impact in every area of our influence while walking in the might and might of the Holy Spirit.

I pray that the 180 days of devotions will provide the groundwork for a lifetime of seeking God's presence and direction. Let us keep in mind as we leave this place that the Lord, who is our constant source of inspiration and strength, is the source of our strength.

Thus, let us rise as men of faith and confidently follow the road that God has planned for us. Let us live our lives with integrity, passion, and purpose, understanding that we are given strength by His Spirit and capable of making a difference in the world.

May God, each day of our life, keep us strong, lead us, and utilize us for His glory.

Dear God,

In your presence, we have gathered here today to ask for your wisdom and support. We are grateful for the chance to gather as men and deepen our knowledge of your Word and faith. We pray for your ongoing presence in our life and your hand of support as we end this devotional.

Father, we understand that being strong means depending on you for support rather than being independent. Please help us to always rely on your eternal arms, knowing that you are powerful even in our weakness. Give us the fortitude to confront the hardships of life with unflinching confidence in you.

Lord, give us the discernment to place a high priority on our connections with our families, friends, and fellow humans. May we always be honorable men who show your strength, love, and compassion in all that we do. Please lead us in all of our choices and deeds so that we could emulate your virtues and positively impact everyone around us.

We offer prayers for every man present today. Bless us individually and as a fraternity. Assist us in supporting and understanding one other during our moments of need. May our solidarity serve as a mirror of your love, and may we draw strength from each other's experiences and testimony.

We give our souls to the Lord, lifting all our worries and anxieties. We beseech you to fill us with serenity, giving us the courage and clarity to face any obstacle head-on. Assist us in fully depending on you and having faith that you won't abandon us.

Finally, O God, we give you thanks for sending your Son, Jesus Christ, to the cross as an example of genuine strength. We pledge to conduct our lives in a way that honors him and are thankful that his blood has purchased the forgiveness of our sins. We offer this prayer in Jesus' name, Amen.